Self-Discipline

The Unconventional Guide to Unstoppable Focus, Mental Toughness, Willpower and Building Daily Habits that Will Boost Your Self-Esteem, Beat Procrastination and Maximize Productivity

Contents

Introduction

"Crock pot mentality always defeats microwave mentality!" — Dave Ramsey

Contrary to what many new age self-help gurus and self-confessed "life coaches" preach, the secret to success is not getting a lot done in a lesser amount of time. It is not about stressing or burning yourself out. It is learning to balance work, leisure, and family life, to lead a more enriched and fulfilling life. Trust me, as harsh as it sounds, in your final hours before leaving this world, you are not going to think about how much money is left in your bank or the businesses you've built. You will think about how happy, content, and rewarding a life you've led, and the moments spent with your loved ones. These are the lovely memories that will flash before your eyes. Not just what you've hustled for and collected over a period of time.

Success is built on a momentum of self-discipline, sound habits, taking action, and investing in yourself. Do not think of it as instant noodles or doing as much as you can in a short span of time. You will burn-out faster. People who make their way to the top fast also tumble down faster. There is a strong philosophy behind "Slow and steady wins the race." You've got to do the groundwork or lay the foundation before creating a strong structure on top. Success is more of a journey than a destination. A journey comprising hardships, learning, modifying your strategy and slowly yet surely building your way to success one step at a time! Ask yourself these important questions – If you get too much success too soon, are you confident of being able to sustain it in the long run? Will you be able to witness the same level of success after five years, ten years, twenty years? Is your learning and development sufficient to help you build on this success for years to come?

Are you happy and pleased with the direction in which your life is headed? Have you achieved the success you are capable of accomplishing, or feel that you deserve? Are you living the life of your dreams and goals? If not, it is time for some reframing and transformations. However, as much as self-help gurus across the world will have you believe that true success comes with doing, doing more and then continuing to do more, it isn't always a quick hustler's mentality that drives you closer to success.

Success comes by slowly and steadily building a foundation strong enough to be designed for life-long glory and mastery. If you want temporary success, by-all-means, chase it as quick as you can. Get after those get-rich-quick schemes lauded by coaches and marketers. However, if you want success that lasts, it helps to give this unconventional wisdom a go. Get out of the instant soup mentality and adopt the stew cooking attitude. Isn't the latter much more delectable? The joy and sustainability of your success will increase once you learn to master the art of slowing down to build one thing at a time, one step at a time. This is not to say that you must halt to inaction or go into slow mode. Don't make this an excuse to feed your procrastination. On the contrary, this self-discipline is about taking slow and steady actions each day to avoid burning out, as opposed to doing a lot all at once and bursting the bubble because you are implementing unsustainable growth. There is only so much time, energy and focus we all possess. Using these resources optimally is the key to long-term success, money, glory, and life-mastery.

You will be surprised by how much you can achieve by making tiny changes in your everyday habits. Tiny steps go a long way in ensuring huge success. These are not just theoretical, unrealistic tips on paper. This is real, actionable, practical advice that has transformed the lives of people across the world to help them lead a holistic and well-rounded life. These are tried and tested concepts utilized by many people to create a 360-degree transformation in their life. The pointers mentioned in this book are dedicated toward streamlining your efforts and bringing more discipline to your actions.

This in turn brings about a positive mindset conditioned for wealth and success. Being successful and self-disciplined starts with the right mindset before it becomes reality. The pointers mentioned throughout this book can bring about a shocking transformation in the way you think, and the notions of success you have grown up believing. They will enhance your energy, positivity, willpower and enthusiasm to get things done in a more balanced and fulfilling manner. All of us possess self-discipline. Much like each person's muscular strength varies; people possess different degrees of self-discipline. Though everyone has it, not everyone has developed it. It takes muscle to create and grow more muscle. Similarly, it takes self-discipline to grow greater self-discipline. Have you used progressive weight training techniques to build muscle? It is about lifting weights gradually until you can no longer lift anything more. You push your body's muscles until they give in, and finally rest. There's always scope for improvement.

This is similar to how self-discipline works. You build discipline by dealing with challenges that can be successfully achieved but they are still near the limit. This doesn't translate into trying and failing each day at something new. It also doesn't imply staying in your cushy comfort zone. You don't gain strength by attempting to lift weights that cannot be budged, nor do you gain strength by lifting weights that are increasingly light. You begin with weights/challenges that are within your current ability, but they are also near your optimal limit.

In Progressive training, you keep increasing the challenge. If you stay within your comfort zone and keep working with the same weight capacity, you aren't getting any stronger. Likewise, if you don't test yourself in life periodically, you don't gain self-discipline. Like a majority of people don't develop their muscles to their fullest potential with proper training, most people do not boast of high discipline levels.

Avoid pushing yourself too much when it comes to building self-discipline. That's not the best way to go about it. You can't transform your life 360-degrees in a day. It isn't realistic to go from being a slack king or queen to a productivity ninja overnight. You can't set three-dozen goals, and expect yourself to meet each of them consistently from day one. It's a recipe for disaster. It is similar to a person hitting the gym for the first time and aiming to pack 300 pounds. It doesn't work and makes you look foolish!

If you can start with fifteen pounds, so be it. That's nothing to hide or be ashamed of. You begin now, from where you currently are. No matter where you are with your discipline (even if you are highly undisciplined), simply start. Begin with little self-discipline goals to build even more discipline. As you get stronger with discipline, the weights or challenges will seem much lighter.

Avoid comparing yourself with others. It will never work. Your expectations will be even harder to meet. If you believe you aren't strong, everyone will appear much stronger. Just look at where you currently are and aim to improve as you move ahead.

Chapter One: Resolve to Change Today

You have a clear choice now before reading any further. Either continue what you are currently doing and live the average, mediocre life you may presently be leading, or tell yourself that it is time to transform and begin taking steps in the right direction from today!

Yes, we will cover proven principles that have brought success to many people. However, change begins with a decision – your decision to lead a more fulfilling life, to be more successful, to give more time to your loved ones and to achieve your goals. The change starts and ends with you. You are holding the steering wheel of your life. No one is in the driver's seat except you. You determine your destiny through your actions and choices. If you want to lead a more wholesome, well-rounded and quality life that is free from stress and focuses on being successful yet happy, this book offers you the much-needed unconventional wisdom required to accomplish it.

Decide to be more self-disciplined, happy, and content. Discover your "whys", and your "hows" will invariably fall in place. All of us have our own, unusual "whys", and the first step toward becoming rich and successful is identifying these. Why do you want to be rich? Maybe, your dream is to travel around the world, which needs a lot of money. You also probably want to give your parents the best possible retirement, or your children the best education, and opportunities in life. You may want to build a dream house or start an NGO that works for the betterment of the underprivileged. You may wish to launch a dance school or train children in martial arts. Possessing a powerful "why" keeps us on track even when the going gets rough. This "why" keeps us afloat even in choppy waters.

Every time you feel like giving up, halt in your tracks and think about your "why". It will help you to keep going.

You've no doubt heard the famous quote from the successful book and movie, *The Secret.* It says, "Thoughts become things." Yes, everything begins with our thoughts and mindset. There is plenty of power in our subconscious mind. We can program our subconscious mind for either greater success or failure by thinking positive or negative thoughts.

Wealth, abundance, and happiness is often just a state of mind. When we think rich and prosperous thoughts, we program our subconscious mind to guide our actions in the direction of success and prosperity. There is a little secret about our subconscious mind that if you know, you can channel to the hilt to achieve your dreams and goals. The human subconscious does not know the difference between reality and imagined reality. Whatever you think continuously is believed to be the truth by your subconscious mind. If you keep thinking you are wealthy, abundant, prosperous and successful, your brain accepts that as your reality. The subconscious mind subsequently guides our actions in alignment with these thoughts. Thus, our actions are directed toward creating even more wealth and success.

Transformation starts within. When you decide to bring about a shift in your thoughts, the process of change occurs. Make a conscious choice to be self-disciplined, think positive thoughts, and work hard toward manifesting your dreams.

If you do what you love doing, you increase your chances of success. When you work on something that you are passionate about, it doesn't seem like work. It feels like you are building your dream, one step at a time. Pick something that you have an inherent interest in, that you are passionate about or that simply brings you joy. You'll boost your chances of success because you'll end up pouring your heart and soul into it. Take any successful person from Bill Gates to Mark Zuckerburg to Steve Jobs to Jeff Bezos – from the start they were all visionaries who were passionate about their work. They were driven by the desire to excel in something that gave them deep personal satisfaction.

When you do something for money, you may be driven initially by the results. However, it may not last long because you don't have an inherent interest in it beyond increasing your bank account. Sustained efforts may pose a challenge if you aren't passionate about what you do. The chances of giving up and finding other ways of making money are high. However, if you are passionate about something, you will have the drive to keep doing it until you accomplish all your goals and dreams because it gives you a feeling of fulfillment.

Also, you may be talented or skilled in your work and passionate about it. However, if you don't put in the right amount of work or energy, you will most likely not witness the desired the results.

Some people possess all the talent in the world. They may also be passionate about their talent. However, they don't accomplish much because they aren't prepared to do what it takes to be successful, by putting in the required effort. Along with a change to your mindset, as well as passion and talent, you need to go out there and sweat it out. You have to be ready to face the dirt, sweat, tears and grime to emerge victorious. As Steve Jobs said, "The people who are crazy enough to think they can change the world are the ones who do." Success starts with a thought, and transitions into consistent effort and actions in the right direction.

Here are some power-packed tips to program your mind for success.

Examine Inner Beliefs

Your inner beliefs and ideas very often set the tone for success or failure in life. The most unfortunate thing about these beliefs is that they are so deeply rooted within our subconscious or psyche that we are often not even aware of it. The ideas may have been planted in your mind through childhood experiences or challenging circumstances or the environment within the family. If your parents burdened you with huge expectations as a child that you were unable to meet, you may grow up believing you aren't good enough for anything.

Similarly, one negative experience in a job early on may lead you to believe that you aren't cut out for a particular career. What does your mental chatter sound like? Consciously identify and examine your self-talk. What are the things you keep telling yourself on repeat mode? Identify the words, sentences and phrases that contribute to any conversations with yourself. Are they positive, hopeful and positioned for success? Or hopeless, desolate, cynical and slated for failure? Overcome self-limiting beliefs and thoughts by reprogramming your mind.

Each time you find yourself coming up with negative mental chatter, stop it in its tracks by performing a physical action such as biting your tongue or smacking yourself on the head or pinching yourself slightly hard. This will stop your seemingly involuntary or reflex thoughts by using physical stimuli. Your inner beliefs and feelings contribute majorly toward hampering your chances of success. Recognize this and crush them to replace unhelpful words with more positive chatter.

Avoid catastrophic or unrealistic thinking, while replacing it with more balanced and positive thoughts. Instead of thinking, "I can never do this", try telling yourself: "Maybe I am not the best at this currently but with time, will, and consistent efforts, I'll master it." You are changing a self-defeatist notion into a more constructive and positive idea that takes you closer to the success mindset. Let a more hopeful belief take control.

Affirmations work brilliantly when it comes to reprogramming your mind from one of hopelessness and failure to hopefulness and success. Affirmations are positive sentences that keep reinforcing your desires in the present, as if you are already what you want. For example, "I am rich, successful and happy" or "I am glad to be wealthy, abundant and successful each day."

Saying these affirmations in a loop or writing them several times (always in the present tense) helps your subconscious mind internalize them. Remember, your subconscious mind believes whatever is repeated several times as the truth. These positive ideas become firmly embedded or imprinted into your subconscious as the only truth. Your mind then gets to work and directs your actions and behavior in line with these powerful positive beliefs.

I like to write these affirmations on notes and stick them where I can easily spot them every day. On my bathroom mirror, refrigerator, work desk, or cupboard. This allows me to keep reminding my subconscious mind about my goals and desires. Are your inner beliefs stopping you from being wealthy? Identify what you most want to achieve and use the power of positive affirmations to manifest this reality.

Build an Attitude of Gratitude

The quickest way to get into a more positive frame of mind is to count your blessings. If you are operating with more negative, self-limiting, and hopeless beliefs, it's time to turn them on their head by being grateful for all the wonderful things in your life. It will bring about a change in the frequency of your thoughts from negative to more positive and hopeful.

Plenty of people (me included) have accomplished a major transformation in their mindset after doing this small exercise. At the end of each day, just before going to bed, make a list of ten things that you have in your life or ten things that happened during the day for which you are truly grateful. If you want to attract more abundance, be grateful for the abundance that already exists in your life. The idea is to feed your subconscious mind with positive thoughts to attract greater positivity.

The idea of doing this just before going to bed is to activate your subconscious mind, which is it at its peak when your conscious mind is asleep. This is why some of the best insights, solutions and "awakenings" come to us while we are asleep. Our subconscious mind is in super active mode. It's not for nothing that they say, "Sleep on it."

Preferably, keep adding a list of ten new blessings each day in your gratitude journal. Trust me, you'll never run out of them. It can be anything from the legs you walk on to the car you drive to work, to the eyes with which you experience the wonderful world around you. Be grateful for being able to walk, smell, taste and speak, for sleeping in a warm bed, and having food to eat. You'll be surprised at how much you have to be grateful for. This doesn't mean you shouldn't want more. It simply means when you are thankful and positive for what you have, your mind will be conditioned to attract even more of these blessings. You are simply shifting your thoughts from negative to positive, to create a more hopeful, "geared for success" mindset.

Meditation and journaling help us to focus on everything that is going right in our lives in order to pave the way for attracting even more of these things. Writing a gratitude journal steers our focus to the positive and helps us renew our vision for ourselves. Begin or end each day with thoughtful reflections about everything that happened that day, or the previous day, for which you are grateful. End every day with small notes about everything that went right, irrespective of how small it seems. These blessings quickly add up to put you in a more positive frame of mind. Invest each day in silent contemplation, meditation, reflection or prayer. This practice brings about a gradual yet definitive shift in the attitude which helps us attract success eventually.

All of this helps to plug into your subconscious mind to connect with your inner self to make more conscious and intuitively driven decisions, which are a big part of self-discipline.

Find abundance in everything you do. This may not be easy. It is tough to think of richness and abundance when you are struggling to make ends meet. However, if you are grateful for whatever little you have, you will multiply these blessings through the power of your subconscious thoughts. This is exactly why some people rise above their circumstances, while others struggle with their "fate".

Build a Wealthy Mindset by Turning Obstacles into Opportunities

Contrary to popular perception, winners are not people who never experience challenges or failures. They are, in fact, people who take these challenges and turn them on their head into opportunities and learning.

When people chided Thomas Edison for one thousand failed experiments before he created the light bulb, he famously said, "I don't see it as failure. Now, I know one thousand ways that don't work." Every failure or obstacle is an opportunity to learn and grow, which takes you closer to your success. Even if things don't go your way, you've now learnt to strike off one strategy and move to the next. You know what won't work. Don't place limits on what you can achieve, and don't limit your definition of success. Learning is also success! When something you tried doesn't work, at least now you know what not to do to be successful.

Everything stems from self-belief. It comes from knowing your true potential and believing in your abilities, despite trying times. Focus on your strengths even in tough situations. In fact, use these obstacles or roadblocks as stepping stones on your path to success.

Let me share an example with you. My friend got the pink slip after his company began massive downsizing operations. They wanted to control their operating costs and decided to axe a few positions. Desolate, desperate and hopeless, my friend didn't know what to do to support himself and his family. After days of wallowing in self-pity, he took ownership of his life and career and decided to go back to college to pursue education that would help him in his field in the future. He and his wife dipped into their personal savings to fund his education. His wife took up a few jobs to contribute to the family income. My friend also did part-time jobs, and continued his education. He graduated, and launched his start-up together with a classmate after receiving funding from venture capitalists.

He toiled hard on his start-up, while also doing other jobs to support his income. His start-up began picking up momentum gradually. At first, he was barely able to break even. Later, the venture started witnessing steady profits until it became one of the city's most sought after enterprises that now does roaring business. Yes, this is a classic example of how an "adversity" was turned on its head into an opportunity. Imagine if that lay off hadn't happened, my friend would have still been a bucket carrier—carrying buckets from nine to five, fulfilling someone else's vision and working at some else's commands. Today, he is a successful entrepreneur and consultant for start-ups working on his own terms, fulfilling his own goals and desires.

Decide to Change Now

Yes, if you are not happy with your life, career, and finances—decide to make changes to your thoughts, habits, actions, mindset, attitude and behavior today. Everything that you need to be rich and successful is within you. It is already lying there inside you. You just have to tap it and unlock it to witness huge success.

Sometimes, we wonder why despite being so talented someone is not able to accomplish their desired success levels, while another person who may not be as talented witnesses roaring success. It is simply a matter of having the right mindset, which drives you to work hard and chase your goals despite obstacles.

If you want something you've never had, be prepared to do something you've never done. Some people keep doing the same things over a long period of time and expecting different results. If you want to transform your life, start changing your approach, mindset and habits. To get something you've never got, be prepared to do something you haven't done yet.

Success is a habit that is largely determined by our self-discipline, by what we choose to invest our time, effort, and monetary resources on. It involves setting goals and actively working toward fulfilling those goals.

Chapter Two: Embrace Failures as Stepping Stones to Success

Yes, there are no excuses for failure! No one except yourself and your self-limiting mindset holds you back. What is your definition of failure? Do you let it get the better of you by giving up? In this case it is your enemy! Or do you learn the right lessons and convert it into a brilliant opportunity? If yes, failure becomes your ally, doesn't it? Are you bogged down by failure or do you have the courage to get up, brush off the dust, and give it a good fight all over again? Like I mentioned earlier, failure can either be a stumbling block or stepping stone. It is your perception of failure that defines your success! Fear of failing is worse than failure itself because it confines you to a life of untapped potential.

No person is perfect. Even the rich and famous people you admire have gone through their share of trials and tribulations to emerge victorious. They've failed too. And many more times than you've even tried! Thomas Edison tried to create the light bulb unsuccessfully in a thousand different ways. Have you even tried something a thousand times? And you wonder why you are not the next Edison, Zuckerberg or Steve Jobs! The difference is these people have the conviction to convert their challenges and failures into triumphs, something which most people don't do. That is why there are only so many super successful people. It's the attitude!

Did you know Oprah Winfrey was sacked as the news anchor of a Baltimore channel for becoming too emotionally involved in the news stories? Her characteristic trait went on to define Oprah's diva anchor status and made her one of the highest paying television personalities of all times! Henry Ford's financers pulled out a couple of times before he produced a passable automobile prototype. The list of successful people who've turned failure on its head is endless. If you want to be one among them, here are some ways clever people utilize failure to their advantage:

1. Acknowledge your mistakes – It takes courage to admit that you screwed up, and that is the first step toward success. Own up to your mistakes and accept responsibility for your actions, rather than blaming other people or external circumstances. When you take responsibility for your actions, you are in control of your life. When you acknowledge your mistake, you hit upon the realization that this isn't the best way to do things. The first step toward changing any habit, behavior pattern, action, thought process, or strategy is to acknowledge that there is a problem. Once you identify the problem, acting upon it becomes easier. For instance, if you realize or own up to the fact that you are not able to save much money because of irresponsible spending habits, you'll take measures to work upon it. Identifying the root cause and acknowledging your failures sets the momentum for future transformation in a positive direction.

2. Keep the right perspective. I'll tell you a little story here that was published in the *Chicken Soup for the Soul* series. There was a pair of identical twins. While one child was a beaming optimist, the other was a cynical and hopeless pessimist. Their parents were predictably worried about this, and brought them to the neighborhood psychologist. To balance their thought processes and personalities,

the psychologist suggested a small yet significant exercise. On their birthday, both were assigned separate rooms to pick up their gifts.

The pessimist entered his room to see it filled with the best toys their parents could buy. There were games, a computer, a toy car, a calculator—pretty much everything a child would want. The optimist, on the other hand, entered a room full of manure. The parents carefully hid in the corridor to note the results of the exercise on the boys' thinking. The pessimist twin complained about the color of the computer and the material out of which the calculator was made. He thought the game wasn't good enough for him, and that his friend had a bigger car than the one he'd been given.

In the other room, the optimist was jumping with joy. He was delightfully flinging the manure up in the air saying, "You can't really fool me! Where there is this much manure, there's got to be a pony!" See the difference? It's your perspective that matters. Do you see failure as a monster that is out to stop your success and abundance? Or is it an angel in disguise that is leading you to the right direction by telling you what not to do now? You can either view failure as a stumbling block or a stepping stone. The choice is yours! And the perspective with which you view failure will largely determine your chances of success.

3. Stay persistent. Few things are more responsible for your success than the ability to stay afloat despite being in choppy waters. You can't cross the ocean by looking at it from the shore. You have to go out there, face the grind, fail, and then get up again to succeed. There will be people who will make you give up on your dreams and say it's impossible. Who knew Walt Disney could create a world like Disneyland?

People laughed at Galileo when he stated that the earth moves around the sun. Popular perception around that time was that the sun moved around the earth, which was believed to be the epicenter of the universe. When people say something can't be done, remember they are referring to their inability to do it, which doesn't necessarily define yours! Persistence is nothing but optimism at work.

When regular people say "That's enough" and quit, winners say "I am not doing enough", and continue. Instead of quitting, they take on challenges with gusto and stay persistent. Despite witnessing setbacks, they stay consistent in their wealth and success building efforts. Like the proverbial phoenix, they are unafraid to rise from the ashes.

4. Your "why" keeps you going. Remember, we'd spoken about having a clear "why" in place before doing anything? Well, your "why" will keep you going even when the "how" becomes difficult. When you have a clear "why" in place, the "how" can be figured out. If you know you are doing something to give your children the best life possible, you will keep going with this purpose in mind, even when things get tough. You won't be tempted to give up because that means giving up on a strong purpose in your life. It is easier to throw in the towel when you don't have a compelling reason for doing something. A strong reason will keep you motivated and afloat even in the stormy sea.

5. Imperfect action is better than no action at all. Plenty of times, people decide whether to swim or not after merely trying to judge the depth of the water from the shore. What if I fail? Really now, the amount of success stories we've missed because we didn't tap into our real potential, owing to our fear of failure, are countless. Remember, taking action is better than not doing anything. Failing is a million times better than not trying. It gives you insights that inaction won't! Even if you fail, you know a different way to do something that will take you a step closer to success and wealth creation.

Let's say you start a social media page and post great content (at least you think you do). You promote it aggressively to reach the right audience. However, you don't receive a lot of engagement or comments on your post. Now, you know you aren't doing something right. The problem is either the followers you are targeting are not a right fit for the page, or your posts are not appealing enough for them, which means you need to change your content strategy. How would you know this if you hadn't created the page in the first place out of fear of not generating enough followers? Now you have insights about what isn't working. Equipped with this knowledge, you can change your strategy and set things right. You'll never try if you are afraid of failure—and you'll never learn if you don't try!

Chapter Three: Hyper Focus on a Single Task

Let us assume you have five flower pots and a single watering can. You want to water all plants but there is obviously insufficient water for all. In your zest to tend to all pots, you distribute the water equally among all pots. Of course, you want all plants to flourish. Now, none of the flowering plants actually grow, because there is insufficient water. Rather, if you would have utilized the water can for watering or nurturing one flowering plant, it would've thrived. This is precisely how our time and efforts should be hyper focused on one task to achieve optimal results.

Similar to the watering can, we have a limited amount of expendable time and energy. If we try to distribute it between multiple tasks at a single time, none of them flourish. It has been scientifically proven that multitasking actually slows us down and doesn't help us get much done, as compared to laser focusing on a single task at a time. Avoid stressing yourself about getting a lot done in a lesser amount of time. It will slow you down, and the results will be far from impressive. Stellar results need laser focus of energy, time, labor and attention. Our brain can only perform limited tasks when it comes to processing information, focusing on a job, and carrying it out to its fruition.

Launch as many business ventures as you fancy. I am not advocating starting or running multiple projects. However, keep in mind that starting new businesses or jobs doesn't take much. It is easy to launch a hundred different things at once and take pride in the fact that you are getting a lot done. The real value lies in successfully completing these tasks or building on them for success. If you take on many things at one time, you are diffusing your limited resources (remember the watering can) to grow ten different businesses, when the limited resources are insufficient for growing all businesses. Are all your businesses launched together growing, providing value, achieving stellar results, and more? Little chance, I'd say.

Apple CEO Tim Cook once mentioned how Steve Jobs very clearly ingrained the message of the need to focus only on what each worker does best within the company. It is easy to keep adding to your job or business portfolio. It can be a huge challenge to stay focused and see one project through to its successful completion. However, this is precisely what the wealthy and successful lot has mastered. Though they have several businesses and sources of wealth, they rarely focus their effort and attention on more than a one task at a time.

Steve Jobs once said in an interview to Fortune magazine that "People think focus means saying yes to the thing you've got to focus on. But that's not what it means at all. It means saying no to the hundred other good ideas that there are. You have to pick carefully." This quote, in essence, sums up the importance of laser focusing – straight from the legendary tech founder's mouth himself.

Henry Ford made some of the most awesome vehicles. Picasso was an ingenious painter. Einstein was exceptionally good at his scientific theories. These people excelled at their craft because they focused all of their attention, labor and passion on one thing at a time. Mark

Zuckerberg invested all his energies on transforming Facebook into one of the world's most sought-after social media platforms, while Bill Gates did the same for Microsoft. It is the same logic that applies in each of these cases. If you are stressed and anxious about being a one trick pony, take inspiration from some of the planet's biggest brands, like Starbucks, Coca-Cola and so on.

You may be wracking your mind hard to come up with names like Warren Buffet and Richard Branson to debate the 'laser focus' technique since they have more distributed business interests. However, you should also know that Warren Buffet spent around twenty years mastering the investment market, while Richard Branson focused exclusively on Virgin music for more than a decade before conquering the airline industry.

See a single project successfully through by putting in all your energy, time and effort into it before shifting to the next one. Do not spread yourself too thin with your limited resources such as attention, energy and time. Otherwise, it may end up with you launching one hundred average businesses instead of one exceptionally good and phenomenal enterprise you can truly be proud of. Most successful people concentrate on mastery. They give one business, job or project everything, before being inspired to grow their legacy.

Do not live under the illusion that if you are doing two things together, you are getting more done. In fact, you are taking longer to finish both the tasks than you would have if you'd tackled them individually. Avoid trying to be "superhuman" and instead focus on being efficient. When you take on too many things at a time, you can't give concentrated focus, attention and energy to any one task. You are likelier to be more efficient by devoting all your time and energy to one task before taking on another.

For example, let's say instead of answering emails and making phone calls at one time (which is switching your brain back and forth and making you ineffectual in the process), that you simply reply to all the emails first and then start returning the calls. You'll perform both the tasks with increased efficiency.

Group all similar tasks together and create a schedule to handle them at one time, instead of squeezing them in frequently with other tasks. For instance, instead of responding to every email that pops into your inbox throughout the day, schedule a time to tackle all emails together at the end of the day or at the start of the next day. This way you won't be frequently distracted from other tasks throughout the day, and can also respond to your emails in a focused and attentive manner.

Similarly, if you plan to meet people who pitch their services to you (vendors, professionals etc.), reserve a specific day or days to meet them instead of having them walk in and out of your office throughout the week. This way you can work undisturbed on other tasks for the rest of your work week. The idea is to group similar tasks together and schedule them at one time, so you don't go back and forth from one task to another, and build the momentum required to complete a single task in a focused, efficient manner. Don't slow your brain down by taking on too many things at a time.

Understand the importance of delegating responsibility. The Pareto Principle says eighty percent of our results come from twenty percent of our efforts. Identify what twenty percent of your efforts are creating the eighty percent of results and spend more time in those pursuits. Similarly, be smart and delegate tasks that are consuming a major chunk of your time, but not adding considerably to the results. For example, if you observe that a major portion of your time is invested in sending mail and paying out invoices, hire someone to do the task for you, while focusing more on tasks that are bringing you results.

In their bid to get a lot done, people end up over-scheduling. At times, we are tempted to take on more than we can handle but that's not always a good idea. Try to be practical, realistic and easy on yourself by scheduling tasks that you are confident of accomplishing in the given time. Don't always attempt to take extra work or overschedule to impress or help other people.

For instance, if your manager or co-worker says they need something done by the end of the day, and you are already neck deep in work, say something like, "I am slightly overloaded with work today, but I can hand it to you by noon tomorrow." You are being honest about your time limitations without saying a firm "no" to doing the work. Don't push yourself to do more than what you can handle.

Master the ability of saying "no" if you have other more important things to do. It doesn't make you a bad person. Respect your time, and teach people to value it too. Over-scheduling leads to increased stress, and reduced productivity.

Also, avoid rushing from one task to another. It'll end up stifling your productivity and efficiency. You'll find it challenging to stay focused, inspired and motivated as you move from task to task at break-neck speed. Instead, allow yourself some down time between tasks. Breathe. Take in some fresh air and allow your brain to oxygenate, go for a walk, listen to music, paint, meditate, or do another mind-cleansing exercise.

Working for extended spells kills our motivation, energy, and focus. After working for a few hours (1-3 hours) our brain starts slacking off, and we get invariably distracted. This is when all of the day dreaming, doodling, and social media surfing happens. The brain is exhausted and seeks some relief in the form of more instant pleasure or gratification-giving activities that distract it from the overwhelming stress and exhaustion.

Here's why multitasking may not be the virtue it is made out to be (busting the multitasking myths).

Our Brains Are Not Programmed for Multitasking

The human brain is built for focusing on a single task at a time, and burdening it to perform many tasks at one time only reduces its efficiency. The brain functions drop, which can affect the result of every task. As per MIT neuroscientist Earl Miller, the human brain is "Not wired for multitasking". When people believe they are multitasking, they are in effect toggling from one task to another rapidly. Think about the number of browsing screens open on your computer at this time. Isn't it tough to get things done if you are constantly toggling between the multiple web pages or applications open on your computer currently? Wouldn't it be easier to look for information and work if you only had a single browsing window open? This is exactly what happens to our brain when it is inundated with tasks. It has to keep toggling, shuffling and shifting between tasks, thus impacting its overall productivity. And each time you end up doing this, you pay a high cognitive cost.

In effect, when we think we are being hyper productive by doing many things at a time, we are paying the price by compromising on the quality of each of these tasks.

Perpetually toggling between tasks reduces the momentum that is created when you concentrate on one task for a longer duration. When you toggle between tasks, the momentum is interrupted, which means you have to begin all over again when you return to the task. Focusing on one task for a longer period channels our cognitive powers exclusively toward the particular task, thus getting rid of cognitive disruption.

Look at it this way – you are creating a structure. You work on it sincerely, giving it all the time, focus and energy it requires, one building block at a time. All of a sudden, something else demands your immediate attention. You shift focus to the new task, while the building blocks come tumbling down. You get back to building them when you have completed the new task.

Now you do not have the same level of energy, attention, enthusiasm and cognitive abilities to build those blocks all over again.

The disruption in momentum that occurs from continuously doing a task and working on it over a period of time interferes with the outcome. When we try to complete a tiny task, like sending an email or replying to a text message, our brains quickly secrete dopamine (a feel-good hormone). Owing to the fact that the brain secretes plenty of dopamine, we are constantly led to believe that switching between small tasks that award us instant gratification is the name of the game.

For example, when you are working on writing a project and you suddenly feel the urge to scan through your social media feed and comment on a few posts, your brain is seeking instant gratification.

The most unfortunate part about this is that this process creates a feedback loop that gives us the impression that we are achieving a lot, when in reality we are not accomplishing much—or at least not fulfilling important tasks that need critical thinking.

Multitasking Reduces Productivity and Efficiency

It is tough to organize thoughts and filter irrelevant information when you multitask. The overall quality of your work suffers when you try to pack in too much within your brain's limited capacity.

Research conducted at the University of London revealed that people who multitasked while doing cognitive exercises witnessed a considerable drop in their Intelligence Quotient. The IQ level drops were similar to the ones people experience when they skip a night's sleep or intake marijuana. Scary, isn't it?

Multitasking also increases the brain's stress hormone – cortisol. When our brain constantly shifts gear between tasks, it pumps up higher levels of cortisol. This leaves us feeling mentally stressed and exhausted, even if your day has just started.

What are the main culprits when it comes to demanding our time and attention? Emails and texts! Several studies have pointed to the conclusion that the constant thrill of checking bolded, unread emails from the inbox, or text messages (which typically demand immediate attention) keeps us forever distracted from focusing on productive tasks.

To avoid this constant pressure, create an email schedule. Instead of having the momentum robbed from your task each time to reply to an email or switch attention to a new job, designate a time to send or reply to all emails together. This way, you are not shifting between tasks every ten minutes. Send or reply to all your emails at the beginning or end of the day (or anytime in between). However, reserve a fixed time for it. Similarly, unless it's urgent (in which case people can call you anyway), resist the urge to reply to text messages until lunch or at the end of the day. This is just one of the several strategies used by the wealthy and successful to stay productive.

If you want to focus on the task at hand, turn off notifications from your emails, social media apps, and texts. Research conducted by McKinsey Global Institute Study revealed that workers spend 28 percent of their working hours during a week checking emails. The multitasking massacre is real. Designate specific timings for each type of task by clubbing similar jobs together.

Multitasking Slows Us Down

Contrary to popular perception, multitasking doesn't save time. It will take you more time and energy to complete two projects if you switch between them, than if you tackle each one separately. This is also true of drivers who take much longer to reach their destination when they chat on mobile phones.

If you really want to save time, avoid multitasking. Instead, perform tasks by grouping them together in batches. For instance, pay all bills online together at one time, or clear all invoices together once a week/forthright/month.

The thing is, every task requires a given mindset. Once you get into the flow of this specific mindset and suddenly take on another task, the brain shifts gear and experiences a change in the mindset to readjust its focus. This takes you longer to complete each job because you've got to keep getting into the groove of both mindsets constantly. Instead, stay on one task at a time and complete it before moving to the next.

Increases the Number of Mistakes

Really now, if you fancy yourself as a superwoman or man who is capable of juggling multiple tasks at a time, rework your strategy. Shuffling between tasks can cause your productivity to plunge by a whopping 40 percent. It can also increase the chances of errors, more so if these tasks involve an increased amount critical thinking.

In a study conducted in France (2010), it was discovered that the human brain is capable of handling only a couple of complex tasks without much trouble. This is due to the fact that our brain has two distinct lobes that can divide tasks equally between them. When you add an additional task, it puts pressure on your frontal cortex, which can result in a higher-number of errors.

If you want to be more productive and minimize errors, focus all your energy, time and efforts on a single task at a time.

You Lose out on Life

Imagine trying to do everything at once and not having the time to enjoy the result of your efforts. Forget about stopping to smell the roses or watching butterflies and the rainbow. Multitaskers don't even see things that are right before them. A study conducted by the Western Washington University in 2009 revealed that 75 percent of college students who strolled across the campus square didn't even notice a vibrantly dressed clown while speaking on their cell phones. In effect, the students were looking at their surroundings. However, none of it registered owing to the "inattentional" blindness - as the researchers termed it. You miss out on being more mindful of the present or experiences in and around you when you are preoccupied with too many things.

Can you focus on your food and eat more mindfully if you are busy sending emails while having a sandwich at your desk? Can you enjoy a walk in the woods if you are busy scrolling through your social media feed while walking? Multitasking takes away the mindfulness and purposefulness from what you are doing. Thus, you are losing out on living in the present or savoring the given moment.

The entire world is waking up to the value of mindfulness, which is nothing but being purposeful and intentional about soaking in the present moment in a non-judgmental manner. By doing too many things at a time, you are not focusing mindfully on a single task. You may be physically present, but you aren't really "in" the moment or mentally present enough to experience it to its fullest. Being mindful means even when you are overcome by the urge to focus on multiple jobs at once, you simply acknowledge these distracting thoughts and redirect focus back to the present or most-high priority task at hand. Instead of pushing these disturbing and distracting feelings from the mind, you simply acknowledge them, allow them to live their time, and then gently focus attention back to what you are doing. Practice mindful meditation to increase your attention-span, concentration, and focus.

Mindful meditation involves sitting in a comfortable posture in a distraction free place to focus on your breathing. Put all electronic devices on silent and eliminate all distractions. Sit in a calm and serene space. Relax your body and mind. Start focusing on your breath. Notice the inhalation and exhalation rhythms. Count and draw long breaths by keenly focusing on every inhalation and exhalation.

Notice the feeling of air making its way into your mouth, throat, lungs, and stomach. How does your body feel with each breath in and out? There will be a bunch of distracting thoughts that will attempt to take away focus from your breathing. However, acknowledge these thoughts briefly and let them pass before redirecting focus to the breath.

Disrupts Creativity and Vital "Eureka" Moments

Multitasking needs plenty of working memory or short-term brain storage. When the entire working memory is utilized, it starts affecting your creativity. This was established by research conducted at the University of Illinois in Chicago. Too much pressure and focus placed on working memory can actually end up harming our performance where creative problem solving is concerned.

Multitaskers are often robbed of intuitions, day dreams and those quick "'Eureka!" moments. There is no spontaneity or moments of revelation because the creativity is clouded by performing too many tasks at a time. You are more tuned in to your creativity and inner self when your brain is not overwhelmed by several tasks.

Thoughts, ideas, and solutions follow freely when you are more connected to your creative, inner self. If you want to bring greater spontaneity in your thought process and ideas, start doing less or focus on one thing at a time. Daydreams, intuition and "Aha!" moments are closely linked with our subconscious mind. When you focus on doing too many things at once, you are breaking the connection between your conscious and subconscious mind, thus robbing yourself of precious spontaneity and more intuitively driven actions or decisions.

Scattered Attention Gives Scattered Results

We are in control of ensuring that our energy isn't diffused on multiple tasks that award us less than flattering results. Remember the flower pot analogy? Stop wasting your attention, focus, energy and efforts! Clump them together on a single activity if you want to increase your chances of success. Of course, at times the situation is beyond our control. We can't do much about changing market dynamics that impact our business or varying trends impacting buyer preferences as an entrepreneur.

However, what we can do is strengthen our efforts by avoiding scattered or fragmented attention.

How do you light a fire? You bundle up the available tinder and light it. You do not go around lighting little fires across a hundred grass blades throughout the field. Focus on that one spark it takes to burn the bunch of tinder instead of trying to light fifty different things at once. Do not get me wrong—rich and successful people do not put all their eggs in a single basket. However, they rarely fill all their baskets to the brim at the same time.

By all means, build diverse income sources, multiple enterprises or investment channels. However, it is crucial to laser focus your efforts, time and energy purposefully on one task at a time. Let us say you enter a gymnasium for the first time. There's a barbell, kettlebell, or any other fitness equipment you fancy before you. There are plenty of thoughts circulating in your mind. What exactly is the weight on that bar? How do I place my feet? Where should my hands be? Then there's a ton of other unrelated stuff going on in your head. Did I lock the house door before coming? When is the project I am currently working on due? Did I deposit the last check I received from the client? Have I worn my t-shirt backwards? These underpants hurt like hell!

Too many thoughts result in scattered attention. Now take all this attention, focus, and energy, and invest them in a single task, idea or thought. Finish it before moving on to the next. Scattered attention will give you scattered results, which isn't the best success policy. You need to give every task you undertake the best chance of success!

Tips to Boost Your Focus and Lower Distractions

1. Build a schedule for distractions.

We all have those niggling little distractions that award us instant gratification or pleasure. Having fun conversations with co-workers, checking our social media feed, listening to music, checking out the latest collection on your favorite ecommerce site. It's achingly enjoyable, I know. However, one of the biggest reasons why some people are roaringly successful while others barely manage to scrape through life, is because the former club has mastered the art of delaying gratification.

Giving in to instant pleasures can cause your focus and performance to nose-dive. Plus, you may not enjoy your pleasurable distractions as much if you do them smack in the middle of an important project (at the back of your mind you know there's something important to be finished). So why not factor in a separate schedule for these distractions, rather than compromise both on your work and leisure? Don't deny yourselves the little joys of life. Instead, schedule a separate time for them.

Once you finish working on the current task at hand or after writing a few pages, go and grab a cup of coffee or catch up with co-workers. When you set clear task completion goals, you will be even more motivated to finish them. It's like bribing yourself to complete a task quickly so you can then go and enjoy your pleasurable little distractions. And having a real break after a longer period of focused attention helps you to come back to the next job refreshed, and ready to switch on that laser focus once again.

2. You are not cooking stew.

There are tons of things that happen to us each day, which set positive or negative momentum for the day. It is human nature to obsess over the negative and keep stewing it in minds. When things don't go as we want them to, we keep focusing on this negativity for extended periods. At times, the small and inconsequential things occupy more attention than they deserve.

You are cooking stew on a slow flame! Things can go wrong but to fuss over them for longer than you need simply expends your time, energy and focus, thus spilling over their unfortunate effects into another task. Stop right there! Don't let one negative thing someone said or did impact all that you have planned.

Your phone may have stopped working or your boss may have chided you for not doing the latest project as well as you did the earlier ones. For the former, instead of fussing over the phone for too long, you take a few minutes to figure out if you can rectify it. If not, you contact the company to look into the issue. When your boss says that you didn't do as well in the latest project as they had expected, you focus on the current task at hand and maybe rework on the earlier project once this one's done.

Focus on what needs to be done, not what is beyond you (phone repair) or something that's already in the past (project). Take action in the right direction or have a plan in place to rectify it when something bothers you, instead of over thinking or obsessing about it.

3. Do not open what you do not need.

Sometimes I see a million tabs open on the computers of people complaining about how they are having a hard time focusing on their work. Buddy, if you don't need those tabs or applications, why open them? Don't log in to your email on the computer if you don't need it while working on something more important. If you don't need to know about the next big flash sale, don't open your favorite shopping site.

Golden rule – don't open anything you don't need while working on your system. When social media platforms, applications and multiple tabs are not open, it is easier to concentrate on the task you are trying to complete on your computer.

The risk of being distracted is even greater when you are working from home or a café. If you are at the café, don't get the Wi-Fi access code if you don't need the internet. You'll be likelier to focus on your work in the face of reduced distractions.

There are several handy applications that can temporarily block your social media accounts to prevent you from being distracted. For instance, SelfControl is an application that allows you to select websites you want to browse for a set time.

4. Make yourself unavailable.

Yes, you are expected to work during your office hours and to avoid distractions. But you should also specifically schedule time when you are completely "unavailable" in order to eliminate distractions. One of my friends who is a manager at a top firm hired a coach to help improve his time management. The first thing the coach asked him to do was to take a couple of hours each day to completely cut off from everything and everyone.

The door to his cabin would be closed, the telephone would be off the hook, and he had to make it clear to his staff that he wasn't available during those two hours unless it was an emergency. Using this technique, my friend was able to accomplish more in those two hours than he would in the rest of the entire day. This is the power of laser focus and avoiding scattered attention or distractions.

Working long hours is terribly hyped. It isn't something one should be proud of. It simply means you weren't able to manage your time and productivity effectively, which is why the hours got stretched. You really don't need to be efficient for the entire eight hours to be a good worker. If you perform at your optimal level of efficiency even for a couple of hours each day, without any distractions, you accomplish a major chunk of your day's work. Focus on the most crucial tasks to be completed while going distraction free or making yourself unavailable, and you'll be blown by how much you can get done!

5. See the task through.

Do you ever feel like you are making superb progress with a task and then suddenly experience the urge to take a break? You can go on that break, which inevitably spans longer than you planned, and then get back to the task. When you pick up from where you left it, you realize you've lost momentum. It will now take you sometime to get into the groove of the task to reach the point you were at when you left for a break. We do this, often unaware, several times throughout the day. A quick phone call, checking social media on an impulse, heading out for a coffee break—at times we don't even consider it a break.

See the task through to its completion before you move on to the next milestone or take your break. This allows you to recharge your batteries after completing one task, and approach the new one with a fresh and rejuvenated mind.

6. Keep an eye on the temperature.

No, this isn't about how angry or cool you are. It is about the temperature of your immediate work environment. A Cornell University study found that the efficiency of workers is at its peak and they tend to make fewer mistakes when the temperature is between 68 and 77 degrees. When it's too cold or too hot, our focus/productivity can be hampered. Another piece of research conducted by the Helsinki Institute of Technology revealed that the magic figure is 71 degrees. You may not be able to control the workplace thermostat. Bring some warm attire or fans!

7. Maintain a clutter-free desk.

It is easy to feel distracted or experience the urge to multitask when your desk is filled with plenty of unwanted stuff. Plus, you'll spend plenty of time looking for something you really need because there's a ton of stuff you don't need. Take the time to organize your desk for success. File all your papers in different folders by categorizing them. Make a place for all the knick-knacks. Don't keep anything you don't need right away on the desk or work table. This will help you stay focused on the tasks that need to be completed immediately without distractions.

8. Train people or set ground rules.

A significant amount of our distractions originate from others. There are constant interruptions, disturbances, and distractions caused by other people in our everyday lives. The smartest way to prevent this and focus our energy on the task at hand is to set ground rules and communicate them clearly to everyone. Politely and assertively explain to others that you would appreciate it if they don't interrupt you and respect your need to focus by reducing communication with you during designated time blocks.

Chapter Four: Define Your "Why"

"If we have our own 'why' in life we shall get along with almost any 'how'." – Friedrich Nietzsche

Yes, you want to accomplish certain dreams and goals, which is why you are going through this book. However, do you know why you want to achieve them? For instance, I asked one of my clients why they wanted to launch a business. He stated in a very matter of fact manner that he wanted a big house, a swish car, and the best vacations money could buy. I repeated my question. Again, he said because he wanted all the material possessions that he already mentioned. I asked him for the third time, and he lost all patience by now and snapped at me. I calmly told him that he was only mentioning material possessions or the means to an end, which were not really his true driving force and end. Then, something struck him, and he quickly realized his folly and said, "Because I want to give my family the best life possible."

What is your "why" that will drive you toward your goals with the right zeal, motivation and enthusiasm? When you define your "why", the "how" invariably chalks its path. You have to know why you want to accomplish something or what is the higher purpose or reason for accomplishing it before you can chase it with all you have. Your "why" keeps you on course in choppy waters, it will help you stay strong and motivated when the going gets tough. Each of us has a "why" that needs to be discovered, and not everyone has the same "whys". Someone may work hard for the bigger purpose of giving their children a good life and education; others may work hard to travel around the world. Still others may work hard because it is their dream to open an art school. Each of us has a distinct "why" that drives us. Identifying your own is the first and most important step to achieving success, wealth and life mastery.

Defining your "why" at the outset is important because each time you are tempted to throw in the towel in the face of obstacles, your "why" will prevent you from doing this. When challenges knock you down, it will allow you to get up, shake the dust off and continue your efforts. Your "why" will sustain you in the long run!

The "why" gives you a value filled, directed and purposeful life. Define your "why" clearly. Why do you really want to do something—financial freedom, more time with family, travel, to help others, or are you just simply passionate about your goal? The "why" is integral to your success! Even when figuring out the "how", the "why" can play a big role. How badly you want something is determined by your "why" and if it is strong enough, you are unstoppable. Being a hustler and "goal digger" comes easy when your "why" is in place.

We've all played video games, right? They are a fantastic analogy for life itself. There are multiple levels, obstacles and energy boosters. Hell, if I put aside a penny for the number of times I've got thrown off the course by the obstacles, I'd own a gold charter plane by now. We face monsters and enemies trying to catch us off guard. However, we don't give up playing. Our resolve to win deepens with every defeat, and we play until we knock down those enemies and obstacles. Life isn't any different really!

If you have a powerful "why", you continue playing instead of quitting. If you have a powerful "why", you will not just try to pass classes but to ace them! With a strong "why", you won't simply work to pay your bills but to have enough to travel around the world. Your "why" will not just help you write a screenplay that gets made into a movie, you'll write an Oscar winning screenplay. The difference between achieving success and excellence or failure and mediocrity is often a "why." If you haven't already defined your "whys", do it now!

You can't calm every storm that comes your way. However, you can calm yourself to prepare for the storm, and the storm will eventually pass.

Knowing your "why" awards you the motivation and ability to make choices about your personal and professional life to gain greater fulfilment in everything you do.

Irrespective of whether you are a businessperson, an employee, a team leader, a freelancer, an intern, a student, or whoever—you want a clear "why" to inject passion into your work. Without purpose or passion, you will be likelier to give up when the course gets rough. Those who operate with a solid "why" possess the ability to not just do great work but also inspire those around them. This is because people with a powerful "why" are very driven.

I'll let you in on one of the most unfortunate aspects of human existence. A majority of people live their life by accident. Things will happen to them by chance. We take things as they come, going with the flow, living in autopilot mode. This is merely surviving or existing, not living. Living comes with fulfillment, which in turn is a result of purpose. When you derive a sense of fulfillment from your purpose, you keep going. You don't simply exist, you live. You don't act to survive, you act to conquer.

Today's work-life isn't a cakewalk. You get up early. Drive to work. Deal with a pesky boss and at times even peskier co-workers. Then you hustle to make money, and spend sleepless nights trying to meet a deadline. Rinse. Repeat. There are plenty of challenges to deal with on a day to day basis.

Why get fancy by trying to also understand why you do what you do? Well, because your "why" will prevent you from functioning on auto pilot mode where things happen *to* you. Instead, with a clear purpose, you will make things happen.

When you identify your "why", you are able to seek greater clarity, discipline and confidence to make choices about your relationships, career, communities and other institutions, that will also serve your purpose. You will aim to inspire and be inspired in everything you do.

Do you want to wake up each morning with an infectious energy, enthusiasm and passion for work? Do you want to get home feeling fulfilled at the end of every single day? The secret is – WHY.

If you've faced a considerable crisis in life, you would have experienced the power of having a purpose. You will tap into inexhaustible reserves of energy, courage, perseverance and determination that you were not even aware you possessed.

When your mission is clear, you'll have laser-like focus. Think of the purpose as the same as sunlight focused via a magnifying glass. When the light is diffused, it is useless. However, when this same light is concentrated, it can set paper on fire. Focus light even more with a laser beam and it can slice steel.

Similarly, a clear purpose lets you concentrate all your efforts on priorities—on things that matter the most. It will push you to take risks and move ahead, regardless of obstacles and setbacks.

What is the major difference between humans and animals? Humans, unlike animals, desire much more from their life than just survival. Without answering the question: "What are we surviving for?" You'll be overcome by feelings of depression, despair and disillusionment if you don't have a purpose!

Ever wondered why there is an alarming increase in the instances of substance abuse, suicide and mental illnesses like depression? Or a growing dependence on anti-depressants? The likeliest reason is lack of purpose and true meaning.

You know you are doing something, but you don't know why you are doing it. People are wealthier today than they've ever been, yet unfortunately there's a huge gap between well-placed and well-being. This is because wealth alone is pointless without purpose.

A new hire once went to the HR manager and stated that he wasn't keen to continue working in the organization. When questioned about his desire to leave, he stated that the workplace was filled with negativity, with people talking badly about each other, engaging in politics and gossip.

The HR manager then told him that he could leave the organization if he fulfilled one task sincerely. He was to take a glass full of water and walk around the office thrice without spilling a single drop. After completing this, the employee could leave.

The new recruit got to work immediately and walked thrice around the office without spilling a single drop on the floor. He went to the HR manager and told him he had successfully completed the task. The HR manager then asked whether he had heard other employees talk badly about each other, gossip or create disturbances. The man replied that he hadn't. The HR manager also asked if he had seen anyone look at him in a negative manner. The recruit again replied that he hadn't.

The HR manager explained to the new recruit that this was because he had a clear goal to avoid spilling water, which was directly linked to his purpose of wanting to quit the organization. The same is true with our life. When we have a clear purpose, we focus on our priorities instead of other people's negativity or mistakes!

All the people I know realize that they've got to work really hard, and many of them work hard. However, only a handful of them know what they truly want to accomplish from the hard work. How do you plan to get anything in life if you don't even know what you want or what you are working for? Will you reach your destination if you don't enter an address in your GPS? Money isn't really a well-defined goal. How will you realize you've made sufficient money to fulfill your goal of simply making "more" money? How much is more? Does this translate into a private jet, an expensive car, or vacations abroad every six months? Setting clear goals—or "whys" —awards you the gratification of knowing that your goals are fulfilled when you accomplish them. Let your reasons be crystal clear and well-defined.

There is no pathway or "rule of thumb" for identifying your "why." What can you offer? What is your main proposed value? What do you care about? These and several other questions will help you discover your purpose. To help you find the sweet spot of your "why", here are some questions to ask yourself.

1. What are your inherent strengths?

In the book *The Element: How Finding Your Passion Changes Everything*, author Sir Ken Robinson aptly states that our true "Element" is the sweet point at which our primary talents and skills merge with personal passion. When a person is in his or her true element they become more productive, instill more value in the world, and enjoy greater personal—and professional—fulfillment. And surprise, surprise—they make more money!

What are the things that you've been good at always? What are the things that come to you with ease and you often wonder why others find them so challenging? Are you naturally creative and innovative, to come up with out-of-the-box ideas? Are you a genius where details are concerned, naturally executing projects that need precision? Are you a gifted communicator who doesn't have any difficulty in articulating or expressing yourself clearly? Are you a diplomat, negotiator, leader, solution-provider, good listener, networker, change agent, or technocrat? What are your natural strengths?

Now, you may or may not be passionate about what you possess a natural talent for. A fine, agile and graceful dancer may not be passionate about dancing. Similarly, someone who has a knack for writing may not be a passionate writer. However, a majority of people do not show aspirations and ambitions toward things they aren't good at. You are less likely to be passionate about programming when you don't possess at inherent aptitude for technology. Get the drift?

Howard Thurman put it across brilliantly when he said, "Don't ask yourself what the world needs. Ask yourself what makes you come alive, and then go do that. Because what the world needs is people who have come alive."

2. How do you measure life?

If you don't stand for something, you'll fall for just about anything! How do you want your life to be measured? Measuring your life means taking a clear stand for something and then aligning your existence to it.

Living with a strong purpose is focusing on things that matter the most to you. Having said that, something that matters most to you will rarely be "things". While some folks have the liberty of swapping the security of a regular 9-5 job to chase their passion, others have short term goals and responsibilities to take care of—paying off a debt, providing for their kids, paying bills, and more. However, you don't really have to choose between money and passion all the time. Sometimes, a plain shift in your perspective and ideas can change your experiences. Identifying your purpose pushes you to accept challenges and stretch beyond your comfort zone to inspire you.

3. What brings you alive?

This is one important question that will get you thinking in the right direction when it comes to identifying your purpose. What is it that makes you come alive? What are the things that inspire you? What is it that lights a fire in your belly? When I say what makes you "come alive", I am not referring to your love of video games or watching your favorite football team or your fancy wardrobe (unless you are a sport professional or stylist). I am referring to a purpose that's something bigger. It is about connecting at a deeper level with what you are passionate about. It is the awareness that when you are passionate about something and put your attention on it, this can increase your influence and positive impact in ways that few other things can. It is taking on endeavors that light a fire in your belly to make a difference.

Of course, you don't have to be the big-ticket inventor or find a cure for cancer (though why not?). This is about discovering a cause that is higher than you but is also in alignment with who you truly are as a person.

4. Where can you add the highest value?

Taking on something you are innately good at but hate doing is not the best route to fulfillment. However, knowing your inherent strengths and merging them to add maximum value through the implementation of your knowledge, aptitude, education, skills, or experience, helps you concentrate on professional opportunities and roles where you have a high chance of succeeding, while also awarding you a high sense of achievement, fulfillment, and contribution.

People tend to undervalue the abilities and skills that they have a natural expertise for. Try to reframe the concept of value addition, by asking yourself "What problem can I help solve within my organization?" What are the problems that you are passionate about solving or that give you a sense of fulfillment while solving? This way, you'll focus more on your inherent strengths and the things you are naturally good at, than trying to overcome your weaknesses.

5. If money wasn't an issue, what would you do?

This is a good question to ask yourself for determining if you are being driven by money alone or also have passion to go along with it.

Money drives a good number of us. However, it may not always be the primary driver or purpose of your life. It can be just one of the many "whys" or a means to fulfill a "why." Your "why" may be to open a cancer treatment research institute or a charity which needs a good amount of money. Look at what you are currently doing and question yourself if you'd still do it if money was not a consideration. Would you? Be honest. If you had all the money in the world, would you still do what you are presently doing? High chances the answer is "no"! If this is your answer, (which means you are a part of the majority), you are feeling stuck in your job. I won't say get up now and become a professional athlete, a ballet dancer, or a runway model—that's slightly unrealistic (though let no one define your parameters of realistic and unrealistic).

However, you need a career and not a job you are stuck in. A rewarding, fulfilling career that you love and that drives you to get up each morning and head to work. When you are in a career you love, you'll give it your best shot, which will increase your chances of success and wealth. Again, if you are a 9-5 bucket carrier, you can't quit everything overnight and run after what you love doing. You'll begin with one step a time, climbing one rung after another, to slowly make your way to the top. The "why" helps you wake up in the morning and give each day your all. Unless you plug into your purpose, and take action toward fulfilling that purpose, your chances of success are dim. When you plug into your "why", the "how" is never a challenge.

If you do something you are deeply passionate about, you boost your chances of success. When you toil on something that lights up your fire, it stops seeming like work. It is similar to building a dream, one task at a time. Pick something that you have a huge interest in.

Combine this with external rewards, a sense of inner fulfillment and value addition, and you'll find your "why." You'll pour everything into it if you are driven by a deep passion and desire to do something. All successful people, from Bill Gates to Steve Jobs, were also visionaries passionate about what they were doing.

If you do something merely for external rewards or money, it may not sustain you in the long run. Prolonged efforts will be a challenge after the initial euphoria fades. You'll probably quit and find other ways to make money. However, if you are guided by passion, your drive to keep going in the face of obstacles will help you stay on course. This is because the passion will bring a sense of fulfillment.

Having said that let, me also reiterate that passion alone doesn't survive for long if it doesn't generate the required results. You may be passionate about writing poems. However, if it doesn't help to support you financially or allow you to lead a decent life, the passion will wither faster than you realize. This is exactly why your purpose or "why" has to be the sweet spot between intrinsic and extrinsic motivators.

6. What past sign posts can I use to define your future?

Go back to your past to discover the gateway to your future. What made you tick as a child when there were no worldly considerations? What were the things you loved doing or derived pure joy out of in your childhood and teen years? Did you derive great joy from playing a particular sport? Or participating in theatre? How about playing a musical instrument, writing poems, or painting? Drawing comic book characters, playing video games, or looking after animals?

I know most of you will want to hit me hard now, and say, "But we can't make money out of all these childhood passions, in reality!" Why not? Ideas and a game plan are the key. I know many successful artists and painters who make a killing by auctioning their artworks. They employ slick marketing ideas and resourcefully tap into multiple channels to convert their passion into a financially rewarding profession. What stops a passionate horse rider from making a killing out of teaching horse riding lessons to enthusiasts? What is stopping you from developing ideas into money making opportunities? Your own inner, self-limiting beliefs! Passion and monetary rewards aren't mutually exclusive. You can have both. There are innumerable examples around you of people who love doing what they do, which in turn helps them make even more money. So next time, someone asks you—or you ask yourself—"Passion or financial rewards?" Say, "both"!

Go back to your past for references on how you can shape your future. What are the things that you loved doing when money was not a criterion? You'll find some truly revealing answers.

A man came across three laborers who were busy laying bricks. He questioned the first bricklayer about what he was up to. "Can't you see I am laying bricks on the plot?" The man then asked the second laborer what he was doing. "I am building a wall", the laborer replied. Finally, the passerby went to the third brick layer and similarly questioned him about what he was doing. Back came the reply, "I am building a church here."

Did you notice the three distinct perspectives? All three men were doing the exact same work yet the way they viewed their work or the purpose with which they were doing it differed. While one saw it as merely laying bricks on the plot, the other's purpose was to build a church. The first worker most likely was the one who was only concerned about his paycheck. He viewed his work as something that had to be completed so he could get paid, then he was the first one to run out once the end bell rang. The second laborer was probably driven by the need to complete his task and derive a sense of fulfillment from its completion. He is the type who would put in some extra time and effort.

However, it was the third laborer who was driven by a desire to create a religious structure, which would bring divinity to the community and increase worship. There was a higher purpose to his work than simply getting his paycheck or completing the task at hand. This higher purpose drove him to be the best in his job. Every brick that he laid was part of a vision of grandiose, glory, and aspiration. He is the type of worker who would do everything it takes to bring his vision to fulfillment.

Here are some questions you can ask yourself for figuring out your "why" if you haven't already found it by now.

1. Why do you do what you do?

2. What excites you about your present job or career?

3. What is your idea of a fantastic day?

4. What does success mean beyond the paycheck?

5. How does *real* success feel?

6. What do you desire to feel about your influence on the world once you retire?

7. What do you dislike about your present job or career?

8. Why aren't you doing something else?

9. What does a typical bad day look like?

10. What are the things you don't really enjoy about your work?

11. What is failure for you beyond the paycheck?

12. What does failure look like to you?

Other than knowing what you want, your purpose can also be defined by what you don't want. When you know what you don't want, you'll know what you are truly chasing, which helps define your purpose in life.

What are you intrinsic and extrinsic motivators?

Intrinsic motivation is behavior that is guided by internal rewards. In simple words, the motivation to do something originates from the individual because he or she feels internally rewarded for it. There are three main types of intrinsic motivators according to Weinberg and Gould—knowledge, stimulation, and accomplishment.

A person may do something because of a genuine thirst to acquire knowledge or to learn more about a subject. Similarly, a person can feel motivated to do something to enjoy a sense of accomplishment or achievement. Stimulation through challenging or interesting tasks that drive us to do our best, are also a form of intrinsic motivation. The rewards come from within us, not outside of us, unlike extrinsic motivation.

Extrinsic motivation is behavior impacted by external rewards such as grades, fame, wealth and applause or praise. This originates from outside the individual. Performance related rewards can drive an individual to action.

To stay on the course of your goals, you need a healthy combination of both intrinsic and extrinsic motivation. You should be internally driven by a purpose and externally driven by the rewards that come from fulfilling the goal. An inner sense of fulfillment, and external rewards, are both integral to the purpose of goal fulfillment.

Make a list of your intrinsic and extrinsic motivators before you head any further.

Remember, each person's definition of success is different, because their "why" is different from yours. For some people, giving their family a comfortable life will deem them a success. For others, it can be the power and ability to touch other people's lives selflessly that will be their version of success. Still others may view going back to college and getting a degree as success. Your definition of success is a good indicator of your "why", so go out and find what, exactly, that is for you.

Chapter Five: Goal Setting Secrets

Setting goals is integral to accomp0lishing what you want. You may have the best car in the world, and the most detailed map to take you anywhere you want. However, if you don't know where you want to go, the best car and map will be useless. You may possess all the skills and resources in the world to fulfill your dreams. However, if you don't know where you want to go or aren't prepared to drive the car (or take action in the right direction), your chances of achieving success are slim. Yes, goal talk can be boring and lack oomph. Who wants to talk about setting and accomplishing goals when they can just go out there and do whatever they want to achieve success? Goals give clear directions to your actions. They help you identify when you go off track, and can get you right back on the path to success.

In the earlier chapter, wc lcarnt about developing a winning mindset by programming our mind for success. In this chapter, we take a look at how we can create clear goals for accomplishing this success. If you are scared of committing to a purpose, you'll be surprised at how fun, stimulating and fulfilling it can be.

Here are some smart strategies for setting and achieving your goals.

Keep Your Goals Specific

The more detailed and specific your goals are, the higher your chances of fulfilling them. You give your subconscious mind a clearer vision to work with, which then leads it to drive your actions in a specific direction. Many people end up setting ambiguous goals to keep them open and realistic. If you don't set specific goals, you won't make much headway in the right direction.

You won't know if you've accomplished your goal or made real progress if you keep it vague. The idea is to feed your mind with precisely what you want, so you know what needs to be done to get there. For instance, think of a vague goal like, "I want to increase my business profits in the next six months." Now even an increase of $1 is an increase. Did you really accomplish what you wanted? Contrast this with saying something like, "I want my business profits to grow by ten percent in the next six months." Now, you have more direction to maneuver your actions.

If you know you want to have a passive income of $10,000 a month in the next two years, you'll know exactly what investments to make and sources of income to tap into to generate those funds consistently in the next couple of years. If you simply want to earn passive income without knowing how much, what do you think are your chances of taking the right steps toward being a successful passive income generator?

Let's say you love blogging about food. Now, if your goal is to make a steady revenue-generating blog that gives you a certain amount of income each month, you will not know how many affiliate marketing programs to sign up, how many advertisers to approach, or how many informational products you need to create in order to make that money each month. However, if you have a clear figure in mind (let's say $4000 a month), you'll know you have to bring in affiliate marketing commissions worth $1000, revenue from e-book sales worth $1000, direct advertising from food companies worth $1000 etc.

This way you'll know how many companies to approach, how many emails to send out, the amount of time and effort you need to spend each day toward creating content, marketing your blog, building a steady base of followers and approaching advertisers. You get the idea? Specific goals help guide your actions in the right direction. Otherwise, you are just grappling with "open" goals and reaching nowhere.

Break Bigger Goals into Shorter Milestones

Let's say your goal is to retire when you have ten million dollars in your bank account. You want to be financially free, and have all the time and money in the world to enjoy your life. Maybe you plan to travel to exotic destinations with your family or run an NGO. Now, you won't make ten million dollars in a day, a month, or even a year (that is, unless you are robbing a bank). However, if you know what your long-term vision is, you'll break it up into measurable short-term goals that will lead to the fulfillment of the bigger goal.

You'll start investing in mutual funds or the stock market or create informational products that help you make sizeable passive income. Self-discipline involves taking concrete and consistent steps toward your goal, one step at a time. Accomplish one milestone at a time by breaking your larger goal into smaller milestones.

Let's say you are participating in a pizza-eating competition. You certainly can't put that giant cheese-burst into your mouth all at once. The chances of finishing off the entire thing will be higher when you cleverly break it up into bits and pieces instead of trying to do the impossible by eating the pizza as a whole. It's the same with goals. Keep smaller and more realistic deadlines for each milestone, while your eyes are firmly fixated on the larger goal.

If you have to write a 42,000 word project in the next two weeks, then there is a high chance you'll wait until the last minute to finish it, if you define your goal or deadline as the last day of the two week period. However, if you break it up into 3000 words each day for the next fourteen days, you'll be on track with your progress. Breaking your long term or larger goals into small sub-goals makes you accountable for completing smaller bits of the larger goal each day, consistently.

Think about it like this, if you measure the gap between where you are currently and where you want to reach, you'll seldom be encouraged to begin. "I don't even have a hundred dollars in my account right now, how can I be a multi-millionaire?" However, it is easier to say, "Yes, I want to be a multi-millionaire. However, let me break up my goals into milestones and focus on making my first five hundred dollars."

Ambitious goals can be unsettling and demoralizing at times. They may intimidate and frustrate you in the beginning. However, breaking goals into smaller milestones makes it more realistic. You are only working on one goal at a time before heading to the next, which is often known as "chunking" in the self-help world. Using this technique, you are only focusing on achieving smaller goals that add up to the big one.

Having smaller goals reduces the risk of complacency. You know you have to earn a certain amount of money every month or year to reach your magic figure after five years. This way you won't wait until the fourth year to start working. You'll take small steps every day to fulfill the smaller milestones.

Make Visual Maps

If writing your goals appears outdated, keep up with these tech savvy times and create visual maps. Committing your goals to paper is important because your mind internalizes them more successfully. Similarly, your sense of accountability increases when you commit something to paper (or social media/blog in the new age).

Make it your practice to create visual goal maps for all your goals (this has worked wonders for me and others who've tried it). Start by drawing a large circle in the middle of a piece of paper. Mention your ultimate goal in the middle of the circle.

For instance, if you want to build a steady source of income through your passion for photography by becoming an ace photographer, mention it in the center of the circle. Now, draw lines originating from the circle and lead them to smaller circles where you mention all the steps that need to be taken to accomplish this goal.

Go clockwise by starting with the step that needs to be tackled first. In the first smaller circle, you may have mentioned buying a professional DSLR, then the next circle can be about signing up for a photography course or updating your knowledge about photography. The third circle might be promoting yourself on social media or creating your own blog as a photographer, or even looking out for gigs in the classifieds column of local newspapers and online classified platforms.

You may ask happy customers to recommend your services to their social contacts until you build an enviable customer base. Other circles on your goal map may include updating your resume and LinkedIn profile, making cold calls to event management companies and wedding planners. This way, in one glance, your plan of action is ready. It is easier for your mind to assimilate visually represented goals, and then begin working on them. You'll know exactly what is to be done to fulfill the bigger goal, and keep taking actions in the right direction over a period of time.

Chapter Six: Adopt Good Habits

Success certainly does not happen by accident. Successful people are created by learning, imbibing and applying good habits. You don't just randomly pick successful people to look up to, do you? You consciously choose people who can be role models for their habits, lifestyle, and characteristics.

As a person aspiring to be successful, you cannot just do whatever you fancy. There is a greater sense of regulation and discipline. You do not succumb to whims. Truly successful people lead by example. If you are not disciplined, you have absolutely no grounds to discipline others.

How do you expect your followers to stand in a queue when you are always skipping the line? Ever wondered why corrupt and unscrupulous successful people inspire similar followers? Be a shining example for people to emulate. Be responsible and disciplined. Adopt a healthy lifestyle.

So, what are some magic habits that will transform you into an inspiring, enthusiastic and effective person or leader? What are those special success superpowers that a majority of successful people possess? Here they are:

Broaden Your Knowledge and Seek Inspiration

A truly successful individual never ceases to learn. They are fervently looking to upgrade their skills, master new techniques and expand their knowledge base. Steve Jobs and Mark Zuckerberg are shining examples of folks who never give up their quest for knowledge, innovation, and resourcefulness. They have shown a palpable zeal for making people's lives easier. Any wonder then that Zuckerberg is leading a company with a net worth of $328 billion? Or that Jobs completely transformed our digital experience?

Begin by creating a list of knowledge areas you would like to focus on growing. It can be anything from industry specific know-how to broader abilities that help you become a well-rounded person. Identify areas of improvement and find avenues to obtain knowledge. Attend industry relevant seminars, conferences, or lunch and learn sessions. Find an inspiring and motivating mentor who encourages you to push your limits.

Simba from the Lion King (a favorite success flick) only evolved into a leader when he was willing to set aside his childish arrogance and imbibe the right lessons from his father Mufasa, Rafiki, and Zazu. Success is not "owed" to you, nor is it a set-and-forget system. It is learnt every day. Successful people absorb knowledge, learning, self-growth and discovery like a sponge. They are always open to learning from everyone around them and from every opportunity presented to them.

Identify your areas for improvement, then take courses, subscribe to blog feeds, read books, watch videos, practice, ask for additional assignments, take more responsibility and keep evaluating your performance.

Be with the right set of people to borrow their energy. Do you have a circle of friends who have the same goals or areas of focus as you? If not, then do you think you will be inspired to achieve your goal by interacting with your current friends? For instance, if you want to be a famous athlete, would you be able to have a close circle of friends that all hate sports? Your immediate friends should be people who inspire you, are able to share your passion and lead you to fulfill a common goal.

Learn to keep an impeccable appearance and well-groomed look. It enhances your confidence and makes you feel great about yourself, which in turn reflects in your posture and body language. Emulate the way people from Fortune 500 companies dress. Observe their flawless grooming and self-assured actions.

Prioritize Tasks

Successful people with solid time management, prioritization and organizational skills are formidable role models for their team, while also being effective when it comes to goal fulfillment. Time management techniques are crucial for ensuring productivity, leveraging time and efforts, and achieving organization focused goals.

If you are only creating priorities and commanding others to focus their time on them, without having the discipline to meet goals yourself, how on earth do you expect your team to be inspired or convinced to follow suit? Successful people have a clear vision. They set precise and realistic goals. They manage their time resourcefully to meet those goals. Here's how you can be a time management ninja.

Know when to say "no". You are not a people pleaser. Unless you are participating in a congeniality contest, there's no need to say yes to everything that comes your way. Learn to prioritize tasks. Give importance to work that is in sync with the overall vision of the organization or group than you do to individual goals. Learn to say a polite yet firm "no" when you cannot take on additional tasks. Segregate high priority tasks from tasks that can wait.

Use technology smartly to prioritize tasks and goals. It can be as simple as filing emails that need to be acted upon immediately with a special label (say a "Need to Get This Done Quick" label), or color coding your organizer app with different colors according to priority. Make time for leisure, exercise and loved ones. When the colors are balanced, you know you are leading a well-rounded life.

Delegate tasks. Unless you are a one man or woman army, you aren't going to achieve much all by yourself. You only have 24 hours in a day like everyone else. Glowing results can only be achieved by smartly leveraging the time, efforts and skills of your team. Learn to assign responsibility. Identify key strengths in team members and assign suitable tasks. A good master is someone who creates several followers, while a great master is someone who creates several masters. Channel the leader in others so you can better manage a large workforce by delegating responsibility, and getting several tasks done in little time. Empowering subordinates is empowering yourself to work more efficiently and achieve better results.

Be Proactive and Action Oriented

If you are a business leader or planning to take on a successful role in business, you are going to deal with problems on an everyday basis. Be a solution provider. Get out of the reactive or defensive mindset, and take control of situations. Great successful people always have a plan. They are not a party to blame games. They do not have a list of ready excuses. Successful people recognize some things are within their circle of control, while others are not. They control things that are within their control and manage things which are not.

Proactive successful people always have long term plans. They anticipate challenges, crises, or changes, and are equipped to deal with them. Mahatma Gandhi, a seemingly frail and harmless looking man, helped India gain independence from oppressive British rule due to a clear strategy of non-violent revolt. He was proactive in coming up with an unconventional plan for opposing the tyranny of British forces.

Think outside the box for solutions. Be a part of the solution rather than grumbling about the problem. Successful people take charge and do things differently. Successful people always plan ahead and are able to anticipate and curb problems before they happen, instead of reacting when issues spring up unexpectedly.

Focus more on the bigger picture than immediate solutions. Be open to change. Replace defensive and knee-jerk reactions with critical assessment. Make well informed and purposeful decisions by effectively analyzing everything. Proactive successful people always lead by their example. They create a business culture that fosters teamwork, integration of skills, collaboration and consultation.

Eat and Sleep Healthy

Avoid eating food that is low on energy and nutrition and opt for more fiber rich foods. Replace sugar-rich, artificially sweetened, and packaged food with healthier options such as fruits, nuts, and vegetables. To reduce your sweet cravings, try and include more sweet vegetables such as carrots, sweet potatoes, onion, and corn, in your diet. Include more whole grains, and ditch refined carbohydrates such as bread, pasta, and packaged cereals.

Cut down carbohydrates and include more protein in your diet in the form of fish, eggs, chicken, beans, soy, and nuts. Avoid zero nutrition and high calorie processed foods such as pastries, cookies, crisps, and pizzas. Whenever the snack cravings arise, fulfill them with fruits, whole nuts, berries, and sliced vegetables (with natural dips like hummus).

Though some fats can increase your chances of specific diseases, not all fats are bad. Your body needs a healthy and balanced dose of good fats such as omega-3 fats, which help to reduce the risk of heart disease and are a known mood enhancer. Bid adieu to trans fats by avoiding fried foods, candies, cookies and the other "feel-good" entourage. They may give you a temporary rush, but will gradually deteriorate your health.

It is true that “You are what you eat”. Eating a well-balanced and healthy diet keeps your mind, body and spirit alert, energetic and positive. Add more leafy veggies to your diet. Round off your meals with fresh fruits instead of calorie-rich, lethargy-inducing desserts. This will keep your brain sharper and more active.

Eat home cooked meals that reduce your intake of sugar and carbohydrates. It will keep you in good spirits, lower your risk for mental ailments, keep you more physically active, boost your cognitive skills and enhance your decision-making capabilities.

Include calcium in your meals for well-developed teeth and bones. Unsweetened yogurt, beans, asparagus, milk, lettuce, broccoli, cheese, and crimini mushrooms are all great for incorporating calcium in your diet.

Stay away from consuming caffeine in large doses. Keep a close watch on your salt intake, as high sodium consumption can lead to memory loss, high blood pressure, heart ailments and kidney diseases. Replace salt with healthier flavor enhancers such as fresh herbs and spices. Avoid salt-heavy canned soups, box meals and frozen dinners. They often contain sodium beyond the body’s recommended limit. Ask for low sodium options if you are dining at restaurants, since eating out almost always means high salt meals.

Eat in smaller portions and avoid eating straight out of boxes. Instead of starving yourself and then eating giant-sized meals at the end of the day, break your eating pattern into smaller and lighter meals every 2-3 hours. Avoid binge eating or eating when stressed.

Make time to savor your meals rather than simply eating in front of the computer or television. Despite time constraints, do not eat in a hurried manner. Eat slowly and gently by chewing your food well. Stick to fixed meal times whenever possible.

Healthy sleeping habits are vital for keeping the mind active, alert and positive. Keep a regular sleeping schedule. Sleep at the same time (preferably early) and wake up at the same time, even during weekends or holidays. Get a minimum of 7-8 hours of daily sleep. Establish calming bed time rituals such as meditation, journal writing, or visualization.

Avoid exposure to all electronic devices at least 45 minutes prior to bedtime, to enjoy an undisturbed and more relaxed sleep. Keep your bedroom calm, soothing and relaxing. Restrict light exposure in your room post-sundown. Do not consume caffeine or a heavy meal just before bedtime. Keep fluid intake to its minimum just before going to bed. These small yet definitive habits will help you sleep and feel much better throughout the day.

Exercise

Exercise not only boosts your energy levels and muscle strength but it also helps you keep your weight in check, while awarding you with glowing health. Consistent and disciplined physical activity enhances the flow of oxygen and blood to the brain. It also increases the secretion of chemicals that are directly responsible for our cognitive functions. There is conclusive evidence pointing to the fact that people who lead healthier and more active lifestyles are less prone to illnesses and live longer.

Physical activities can give you an instant emotional lift. It helps you thwart emotional exhaustion after a highly stressful day. A single gym session or few minutes of brisk walking can immediately elevate your mood by stimulating brain chemicals, to make you feel more relaxed and positive. A fantastic by-product of a regular exercise routine is that you look great, which in turn enhances your confidence and self-esteem.

Exercise need not be all boring. Take on fun and stimulating activities such as dancing, cycling, swimming, aerobics, playing volleyball and more. If nothing else works, just go for a brisk walk or run in your neighborhood park or enjoy skipping with a jump rope. Competitive sports and martial arts are also a good way to pack more punch in your exercise routine. Your heart rate goes up when doing a physical activity. This invariably makes you feel good.

Regular exercise gives you stronger muscles and physical endurance. The risk of back, joint, and muscle injury reduces considerably. Physical activity also enhances the body's overall coordination, flexibility and balance. Exercise helps direct more nutrition and oxygen to the muscles, thus giving you more energy for performing everyday tasks.

Meditation and Spirituality

Meditation is a powerful stress buster. It slows you down, reduces stress and ensures complete relaxation. It is also a terrific anxiety beater, which means you will be less prone to worrying about the past and future, and can enjoy your present. Meditation or spirituality allow you to connect with your real self or a higher power, and to gain greater self-awareness and self-realization, to live a more fulfilling life.

The virtue of meditation lies in the fact that it primarily shuts down our external layers, such as our judgmental and over-critical brain, to make way to connect with our unconscious thoughts. The chaos of the conscious mind is temporarily cleared to help us connect with deeper layers of our consciousness, tap into inner peace, inspire greater creativity, help us get in touch with our inner child, enter a deeper state of peace, and experience joy. The magic is in slowing down, silencing the chatter of the conscious mind and tuning in to deeper realms of our consciousness.

It has been consistently proven through several studies that meditation is highly effective for managing stress, anxiety, depression, chronic pain and emotional reactions. Meditation offers several physical, cognitive, psychological and spiritual benefits. It helps you enhance your intention, accept what you cannot change, be non-judgmental and focus on the current moment.

Focusing on one object or idea improves clarity, helps you disconnect and empowers you with greater mental clarity for making better decisions. You will be surprised by how much calmer, more balanced, and harmonious you feel from within. A calm mind and sharp thinking helps successful people in challenging situations. Meditation is also known to be boost creativity, lateral thinking and balance. It increases empathy, and enhances team spirit by fostering a feeling of belongingness.

Meditation is not always the strict and inflexible discipline it is made out to be. You can practice it just about anywhere, on a daily basis, to experience its benefits. You can meditate in your office, cabin, outside, or in the car. Begin by practicing deep breathing for a few minutes in the day. This can be followed by mindfulness or visualizations.

Mindfulness Meditation – Start by sitting in a comfortable position in a quiet, distraction-free place. Light a few incense sticks or candles to make the space more positively energized. Wear comfortable clothes and sit in a relaxed position. Close your eyes. Start with deep breathing. Inhale by slowly counting from one to four, then exhale while slowly counting from one to four again. Focus on only on your breath. Notice the feeling of air entering your body through the nose, throat, windpipe, lungs, diaphragm and stomach. Observe the feeling of air entering different parts of your body. Note how your body and mind feel each time a fresh breath of air enters the body.

The idea of mindfulness is to stay focused on the present more purposefully and non-judgmentally. Even if distracting thoughts originate in the mind, don't force them out. Briefly acknowledge them and let them pass. Don't label your thoughts. Notice them and let them move on. Practice mindful mediation for ten to fifteen minutes each day. You don't need a fancy meditation room. Even a disturbance-free office can work fine if you want to quieten your mind in the middle of a busy day.

Loving Kindness Meditation – Begin by closing your eyes and feeling relaxed. Allow your heart to be filled with benevolence, compassion and love. Start by showing yourself loving kindness. Let your heart be filled with love for yourself. Progressively move on to develop loving kindness toward your friend; a neutral acquaintance; a difficult person; then all these at once and subsequently, the whole universe.

This practice can be enhanced by reciting certain words, phrases and sentences that create a powerful feeling of warm heartedness. You have to experience a huge sense of happiness and well-being. This is a good time to say affirmations that reveal your love for yourself. Send love to everyone around you, and wish them peace, abundance and happiness. This will change your own mindset by making you feel more abundant and positive.

Guided Visualization Techniques – Guided visualization or imagery techniques comprise imagining a specific sequence of mental images through the intervention of a trained instructor or teacher. The generation of mental images impacts the mind and body by stimulating sensory perceptions, such as movements, sights, smells, sounds and tastes. It helps a practitioner relax, eliminate negative thoughts, feel more mentally charged and receptive. If you are not practicing with an instructor, you can play guided visualization or imagery videos from YouTube. Practicing guided visualization in the middle of a stressful day will help you to de-stress and feel relaxed. It helps calm your mind, which becomes a powerful channel for creative thoughts. Imagination and creativity flourish when we are in a calm mental state. Master the practice of connection with your highest vision, goals, or sense of purpose in mind. If you cannot figure out what your ultimate vision, purpose, or goals are, do not stress yourself out. It will occur to you eventually when you connect with your inner self.

Mantra Meditation – Mantra Meditation (the Hindu form of meditation) is practiced by chanting a word, sound, syllable, or phrase in a loop. The sound may not have any specific meaning.

However, the idea is to keep your thoughts purposeful and focused! A mantra is not the same as an affirmation. It is a sound that has relevance, owing to the vibration associated with it, along with its meaning. Some masters also believe that the word isn't relevant here; it is the act of using the mind as a tool of focus that matters.

Tops Tips for Beginning a Fulfilling Meditation Practice

1. Understand that meditation is not a compulsion. It is primarily a relaxation technique that has to be done as per your convenience. Pick any time when you won't be disturbed or will have greater freedom to relax and rejuvenate. Keep it flexible. Though the time around sunrise and sunset are considered ideal for practicing meditation, you can practice anytime that suits you.

2. Meditate on an empty stomach. Meditation is generally recommended on an empty stomach. The reason—you may very well go off to sleep if you meditate after a heavy meal. Similarly, if you are starving, you may not be able to focus on it. As a rule of thumb, meditate a couple of hours after eating your meals. This way you are neither too stuffed nor starving.

3. Come back slowly and gently. When you finish your meditation, avoid being in a hurry to move back into the outer world instantly. Instead, give yourself time for the transition. Open your eyes slowly and develop a gradual awareness of your surroundings. Move slowly before you are ready to take on your day!

4. Start with a few deep breaths. Irrespective of the type of meditation you are practicing, start with deep breathing. Taking a few deep breaths helps to steady the pace of your breath, and drives the mind into a more tranquil, meditative state.

5. Brainstorming sessions. Every day I devote a few minutes for my brainstorming sessions. This isn't the same as brainstorming with others or meditation. This is your personal ideating and creativity time. Think of various ideas and opportunities that you can tap during the day, week, month or year. Calm your mind, sit in a

distraction free place and think of ideas. For example, if you have a blog, you may want to think of different content ideas or various ways through which you can monetize the blog. Keep an idea book handy to note down all ideas so you don't forget them later. Keep reading these ideas frequently, so your mind is reminded about working on them. Meditation facilitates the idea creation and imagination process because it silences the mind from unnecessary clutter, to give you more focus and clarity to build on your ideas. Think of solutions to problems and implementation of opportunities. You can play soothing music in the background to facilitate the creativity and imagination.

Spend Time with Family and Friends

Spend time connecting with your loved ones for a good work-life balance. It keeps you relaxed, de-stressed and balanced. New technologies have simplified our tasks to save work time, though they demand a 24/7 response. It is tempting to reply to that mail when you are dining with your family at a restaurant. However, avoid being "enslaved" by technology.

Keep aside a fixed "family or friends" time where you turn off all work-related notifications to connect with loved ones and enjoy leisurely pursuits. Be clear about not answering emails after work hours. Spend a few extra hours on weekdays to complete your presentation, for example, but try and keep weekends free. Ensure you enjoy at least one meal throughout the day with the entire family. Reserve weekends for outings and bonding with the family over watching movies, playing a sport, going camping, enjoying a backyard barbecue or other recreational activities.

Isn't it paradoxical that the very people we work so hard for get the least time with us, and witness our most stressed side? Ensure your family life and personal relationships do not suffer in your pursuit of material goals.

Chapter Seven: Time is Money

"Every day is a bank account, and time is our currency. No one is rich, no one is poor, we've got twenty-four hours each." — Christopher Rice

The first thing I ask a person if I want to determine their mindset and personality is how they utilize their spare time. Ask this one question to people if you want to determine whether they are slated for success or failure, and you'll be stunned by the insights. Winners will always use their time wisely, investing in learning, passion, knowledge, and skills. The average Joes, on the other hand, will spend their time binge-watching shows on Netflix (not that I am not a fan, but I am certainly not addicted), playing games on their console, or surfing the web aimlessly for hours. Not to mention refreshing their social media feed each minute.

Time is money. We all have 24 hours, it is what we do with those 24 hours that makes all the difference. Here are some of my best time management secrets.

A university professor has three different bags of sand, pebbles, and huge rocks, along with a bucket. He requests a volunteer to empty all three stone grades into the bucket. A student steps up to carry out the task meticulously. He starts with the sand, followed by pebbles and rocks, unable to fit everything all in the bucket.

The professor then turns to the class and says, if only he'd put in the rocks first, followed by pebbles and sand, everything would've fit in. Time management is pretty much the same—organizing your pebbles, sand and rocks to fit it all in. Focus on completing your biggest tasks first to leave room for mid-sized and small ones. When you focus on the smaller tasks first, there is a tendency to spend more time on them than needed, leaving little time for performing medium and big tasks efficiently.

Time management is all about planning and organizing your time to accomplish optimal productivity. If you don't plan time slots for large tasks (or rocks) then the small and medium sized tasks (or sand and pebbles) will take all of your time.

Time is wealth. Everyone has 24 hours in a day, yet successful and wealthy people are able to leverage the power of their 24 hours to do much more than people who complain that they "Never have enough time" to do anything. The way that we utilize our time makes all the difference.

How do some people always manage to complete their tasks and even find time for leisure activities while others struggle to meet deadlines? How are some people always ahead of their schedule while others grapple with things at the last minute? It is all a game of slick time management. How you utilize the 24 hours at your disposal—to pack in as much productivity as you can—makes all the difference.

Effective Time Management

1. Divide your tasks into four quadrants. You have twenty different tasks to do but don't know which one to begin with or finish first. Prioritization of tasks is the key. This is a simple yet highly effective method when it comes to prioritizing tasks. Doing this every

morning or before going to bed each day will help to simplify and clarify your schedule for the day.

Make four quadrants in your notepad: 1) Urgent and important. 2) Important but not urgent. 3) Urgent but not important. 4) Not important and not urgent. Next, categorize every task based on each of these four quadrants.

Let's say you have a client presentation coming up in the next couple of days. It's an important account, and you will bag a huge contract from the client if done right. So, working on the presentation is important and urgent. These tasks should be your first priority, since they are both time-bound and crucial. Don't put them off for later. Tackle them as soon as possible.

Next, come tasks that are important yet not urgent. A client may ask you to submit a rough draft before beginning a project. It may not be a time-bound task but it's still important and needs to be completed before you begin working on the project. This makes this an important and not urgent task, which should be next on your priority list after tasks that are both urgent and important.

Now, a restaurant whose hospitality you enjoyed last night may ask you to fill a feedback form and return it before tomorrow, for filing in their records. The task seems urgent because it's time bound but is it really important for you? Not really. These are tasks that are urgent but not important and should be third on your priority list.

The urgent yet not important items can be delegated to someone else, as they are urgent though not important. It doesn't matter if you don't do them yourself. Spend time and energy on completing tasks that are urgent and important, while delegating the not important yet urgent tasks to someone else. This is how smart and successful people leverage their time. They spend their time and energy on high priority and important tasks. Leverage the time and effort of other people to get more done.

Finally, tasks that are neither urgent nor important can wait until you complete tasks from the other three quadrants. For example, completing the next two levels of a virtual game your friend has challenged you to is neither urgent nor important. It can wait until you've completed the more urgent and important tasks.

Make it a habit to do this every day. At the end of the day, go over the entire day's activities to tally every task against the four quadrants. At the end, note which quadrant tasks you've spent maximum time completing. If you are spending time on the tasks that are not important (third quadrant) or that are neither important nor urgent (fourth quadrant), you need to get your priorities in place.

Start each day by creating a list of two to three tasks that are both important and urgent (first quadrant) before moving on to other categories. As you finish each task, tick it off on the list to award yourself a sense of fulfillment and accomplishment, which can inspire you to do even more.

I've found a lot of success when it comes to prioritizing what needs my immediate focus or attention using the four quadrant method. Yes, it has been sufficiently established by now that doing too many tasks at a time isn't a very good idea and laser focus can help you win the day.

2. Be an early starter. Check with any rich and successful person what their time management mantra for success is, and they'll most likely say they are a 5 a.m. person. Be that 5 a.m. person yourself and get more done by beginning early. It has worked wonders for me and several other people. Going to bed early and awakening at 5 a.m. has plenty of benefits other than health. You'll begin early and get a major chunk of your work done by noon, which means you are comfortably on track with the day's tasks. Besides, packing in more during the early part of your day will keep you motivated, charged and positive all through the day. This will get you to do much more during the day. Once you finish a major part of your work by noon,

you'll feel inspired to keep going, which will result in greater productivity.

3. Another efficient time management hack if you have plenty of things to do throughout the day, is to take on the most challenging and time-consuming tasks first. Once you complete the day's most long-winded, time intensive and difficult tasks, it will set a positive rhythm for other tasks, which are way easier than what you just tackled. You'll feel more spirited, motivated and energetic about completing the other jobs.

Also, if you know you have a very long day ahead the next day, grab enough sleep by going to bed early. You'll wake up fresh, enthusiastic and positive. These small tips will go a long way to boost your overall productivity.

4. Use the Pomodoro Technique for time management to enhance productivity. This one's a gem worth trying. The method was created by Francesco Cirillo in the 1980s. "Pomodoro" means "tomato" in Italian, and since Cirillo used a tomato shaped timer to practice his technique as a student, it became known as the Pomodoro Technique.

The way it works is this: you set a timer for 25 minutes and work on the task at hand uninterrupted for that whole time. Once a single pomodoro cycle of 25 minutes is completed, you take a short 3-5 minute break, before beginning the next pomodoro cycle of 25 minutes. Once you finish four such pomodoro cycles of 25 minutes each with a break of 3-5 minutes between each cycle, you take a 15-30 minute break.

If a task is completed before your 25 minutes are up, you invest the remaining minutes in reading, research and learning. Everything else has to wait until you complete your current cycle.

The objective of this ingenious time management and productivity optimization method is to keep you focused and effective. It aims to end distractions and pointless multitasking that hampers productivity. When you do a task undisturbed for 25 minutes, there is a more efficient and uninterrupted momentum and flow, along with more focus and continuity. Breaks also make you feel refreshed, and help you gain better focus and clarity once you are back. Using the timer brings about a sense of urgency, where you focus on completing the task without any distractions. The method helps in developing willpower, focus, and self-control.

5. Use the famous "two-minute" rule. It states that if a task can be completed in less than two minutes, it should be done immediately. The creator, Steve Olenski believes that if we finish something right away, it'll take less time in comparison to putting off the task for later, and then picking up momentum from there.

6. Leverage time, labor and skills smartly. Like everyone else, you have only 24 hours in a day. If you work alone for those 24 hours, your capacity to make money per hour is going to be limited to 24 hours alone. However, smart income generators realize the power of leveraging the time, labor and skills of other people to increase their income. You may not be able to handle all the work alone, especially if you are looking to scale up your business. Delegation of administrative and specialized tasks becomes integral to the success of your organization. If you work alone (even around the clock), you won't be able to put in more than 24 hours a day! However, if you employ four people and each of them puts in eight hours each, you have a whole thirty-two productive hours! Smart leveraging of time, labor and skills is integral to the process of building wealth.

7. Have everything ready the day before. Hasn't it happened several times that you've woken late and grumpy and feel completely out of control with how things are spiraling? You may have an interview or important presentation lined up, and now you are going to be late. The hunt for the pen drive and file begins, and life feels like one big mess! The best remedy to avoid this is to get everything ready the previous day just before going to bed.

If you are writing an important report the next day, have all your research documents ready so you can begin straightaway with the research and writing rather than wasting time looking for documents in a pile of papers. Similarly, have your clothes for the presentation or meeting ready. Having your documents, clothes, files and other things sorted the previous day saves time and allows you to quickly get to the task without stress. You will avoid spending the additional fifteen to twenty minutes searching for things.

8. Do you know the 80-20 Pareto principle? It says that 20 percent of tasks contribute toward 80 percent of our results. Identify those 20 percent tasks that are responsible for 80 percent of your productivity and increase them. Also identify and eliminate time wasters that do not add value to your overall productivity or goals. Checking your social media feed, browsing the net aimlessly for hours, watching television, playing video games etc. can be highly addictive time suckers. Recognize if these time suckers are gobbling a major part of your time, and use that time consciously for more productive activities.

Let's say you invest 20 percent of your time into giving presentations to clients that bring in 80 percent of your overall sales revenue. And you are using a major chunk of the rest of your time drafting emails that are contributing a tiny percentage to the overall sales figures. The millionaire mindset here would be to identify the task that is bringing you more money and keep increasing it, while hiring other people to do tasks that are making small additions to your overall sales figures. In this case, you start giving more presentations and hire someone to send emails.

Combine time-consuming activities or tasks and tackle them together. There are plenty of time-consuming activities to be handled throughout the course of day/week/month's work. Instead of doing them at different times throughout the day or week or month, club them together at once at the designated time. For instance, don't pay each invoice as they keep coming throughout the week. Reserve one day of the week for clearing all invoices together. A huge part of our daily time is spent in responding to emails. This is a huge distraction in the middle of other tasks. If it isn't urgent, designate a separate time for sending and receiving emails at the end of the day rather than responding to an email each time your phone beeps when you are doing something else.

9. Get rid of time suckers and bad habits. I will suggest a quick exercise to help you identify where the majority of your time is invested. Do the seven-day audit. What are you doing currently? Record it in a phone app or journal. You can break it into 30 or 60 minute blocks. Did you get a lot done? Was it time effectively spent? Did you waste time? If you are using the above mentioned four quadrant method, categorize everything you do based on the four quadrants. At the end of the week, tally all numbers. Where was the majority of your time spent? Which quadrant did you most occupy? The insights may surprise you!

Bad habits are one of the biggest time wasters designed purely to kill productivity. The most unfortunate thing is that these time wasters come attached with the illusion that we are getting a lot done. For instance, you may aimlessly browse the internet under the notion of doing research or looking for ideas. Is it adding real value to your overall task?

Binge-watching Netflix, surfing social media incessantly, playing virtual games, or going for drinks with friends frequently, are all negative habits that take away from the valuable little time resources we have. Utilize your time judiciously if you are keen about accomplishing your goals. The big difference between winners and losers is that the former manage to delay gratification and focus on the task at hand, while keeping their vision on the bigger picture. They are keener on long term rewards, which pushes them in the direction of their goals through the productive utilization of time.

All of us envy the rich, successful and famous, yet we aren't prepared to go through the struggle they go through and the things they give up to reach a certain position or level of success in life.

There is plenty of hard work, sacrifice, delayed gratification, and blood and sweat behind the success. And then you wonder why you aren't as successful as the people you admire. Are you prepared to give up your bad habits and delay gratification like them? Are you prepared to be productive and hustle everyday like them? Do you have it in you to delay short term gratification in exchange for long term rewards? Use your time wisely if you are serious about becoming successful and wealthy.

You aren't accomplishing anything by watching Netflix (other than making Netflix richer) unless you are a script writer or movie maker fishing for ideas. Channel every minute toward productivity. If tasks get too overwhelming, take a break.

Have you read Charles Duhigg's book titled *The Power of Habit?* In the book, he describes keystone habits that hold all our other stones. These keystone habits don't just help draw other good habits to you but also help to get rid of bad or unproductive habits. By focusing on keystone habits, you learn to manage your overall time effectively, which makes the process of habit development easier.

All the same, it is important to train and nurture the other side of your brain. Spend time pursuing things that are outside your comfort zone. If you are a medical practitioner, go out there and learn to dance. A violin player can learn kickboxing or taekwondo. Go beyond your predictable comfort zone to explore newer hobbies and pursuits to boost your chances of success. You end up expanding your brain's capacity, while also acquiring new skills in the bargain.

10. The magic of five-minutes. This is one of the most effective strategies for people struggling with procrastination. The Five-Minute Miracle is about questioning yourself along the lines of "What action can I take in under five minutes today that takes this task even a tiny bit ahead?" Once you've nailed down what that one small action is, set your timer for five minutes. Spend the next five minutes exclusively on the task. According to research, once you just

begin something, you are more likely to do it. Instead of simply contemplating doing something, start with the tiniest bit of action.

This psychological principle is referred to as the Zeigarnik effect. It says that unfinished tasks are likelier to get stuck in a loop in our memory. This is exactly why things we didn't do play in a loop in our thoughts. Even the smallest action is action after all. Five minutes makes a world of difference!

You can also try the power-hour technique. A power-hour comprises putting away all distractions and working single-mindedly on a task. As with the Pomodoro Technique, start by putting in concentrated blocks of time (twenty minute blocks). This is followed by brief periods of rest for leveraging uninterrupted time to optimize brain and body function.

Research has proven that the human brain naturally moves through peaks and trough cycles. To optimize our productivity, it is important that you respect the peaks and troughs by balancing focused, dedicated time with integrated leisure and relaxation.

11. Another trick that works wonders when it comes to beating procrastination is working on what you have been putting off as a rough draft. Let us say you want to create an authority blog about weight loss for women, populated with several information-rich blog posts, reviews and stories but find the process of creating this blog from scratch highly overwhelming and intimidating.

The key is to prepare a rough draft, which is comparatively less stressful, tiresome and overwhelming. You start by brainstorming ideas about what you want to include in the blog. These might include key blog topics; personal stories from readers; weight loss supplement reviews; a forum where women who are looking to lose weight can support, inspire, and guide each other; and so on.

Creating a rough draft will free up plenty of energy previously spent on hesitation, uncertainty and pressure about completing the entire task. Each time I am overcome by procrastination, I get down to scribbling key ideas to get started without the burden of doing something big. Tell yourself that it is only a rough draft.

Psychologically, you are tricking your brain into thinking that it isn't real. If our brain believes the task is not for real, it won't experience the same pressure as it does during crucial tasks. The next day, start off from where you left off with the rough draft gradually. Start with one to two blog posts a day. Finalize, edit, and rework them (or any similar action) before sending or publishing them. Wham, you just did something you believed you couldn't. Now you have a weight loss blog with a couple of blog posts. Not bad!

Next, tackle the next two blog posts based on your rough drafts, polish and publish them. There, now you have four information-rich blog posts. Keep going back to your rough draft for inspiration. Once you create a mock-up or rough version, you are likelier to complete a goal to its fruition.

Benefits of Being an Early Bird

We discussed earlier in the chapter on time management about the advantages of being an early riser, and how you can get plenty done by rising early. It's not just another zen habit but also an amazing productivity hack when it comes to getting a lot done.

Fabulous beginning to the day – When you arise early, you'll jump out of the bed and start your day with a bang! When you sleep late, you awake late and start your day in rush mode. Everything is done in a hurried and stressful manner, thus hampering not just your productivity but overall state of mind. You may reach work late, start late and finish late. You may walk into work in a ruffled state, eyes barely open and grumpy. This isn't the best beginning to your day. Now, contrast this with awaking early. You'll get a nice head start, and begin your day on a positive note. In the experience of most successful people, there is no better way to begin your day than to waking up early.

Visualizations, affirmations and journaling – You are freshly awakening from the realm of your subconscious into the conscious mind, which is the best time to journal (dream journals are best written as soon as you wake up), practice guided visualizations and say your affirmations. Start by closing your eyes, and imagining your goals as if they are fulfilled. If you want to be a wealthy person, start visualizing your goals in explicit detail. How are you dressed as a millionaire? How do you walk and talk as a millionaire? How do people react to you? How does your workplace look? Visualize your dream home and car. Where do you go on vacations?

Live these visuals in your mind before manifesting them in reality. This is an important and highly overlooked goal accomplishment process. Practice visualization exercises for ten minutes about twice or three times a day. When you imprint ideas of abundance and success into your subconscious mind, your mind becomes attuned to identifying opportunities that bring even more abundance your way. When your mind is fixated on gratitude, positivity, goals and abundance, it is cut off from self-limiting, destructive and negative thoughts that act as obstacles to your success and abundance.

Make your visualizations a sensory experience by imagining sights, sounds, sensations, tastes and more. This is a powerful practice in internalizing your goals. It sends graphic visual messages to your subconscious mind, which it believes to be real. Your actions are then aligned with these positive visualizations. Make the visualization even more power-packed by repeating affirmations in a loop. You can also write in your gratitude journal or meditate. Spend the early hours of your day on reflection and internalization of your goals.

Make a list of the day's tasks – This is the best time to line up tasks for the day based on the four quadrants explained in the previous chapter. Schedule the most challenging and lengthy tasks for the first half of your day.

Solid Tips for Being an Early Bird

1. If you have a habit of awakening late into the morning, avoid making any sudden drastic changes. Start by awakening 15-30 minutes before your usual time. Get used to this pattern for a few days before making a change of another 15-30 minutes earlier until you reach a comfortably early rising time. Cut back your sleeping time gradually.

2. Sleep early. This one's a no-brainer yet people fail to capitalize on it. Don't stay up late playing games on your phone or watching television. If you sleep late and awaken early, you won't get enough sleep, which will make you snappy and irritable, not to mention unable to focus on your task. An average human adult body needs to rest for at least eight hours a day. Ensure you get enough sleep to optimize your health, productivity and performance.

3. Place the alarm clock at a distance from your bed. If the alarm clock is within your reach, you'll most likely hit snooze and go back to sleep. However, if it is far from your bed, you'll be forced to get out of your bed and turn it off, by which time: bingo! You're already up.

4. Use the extra time resourcefully. I know some people who will wake up at five, only to surf the web pointlessly for a couple of hours. That doesn't give you a jumpstart unless it's related to your work or a part of your media profile. Make it a goal to utilize the additional time well. Prepare your lunch, read a book, go through your report for any corrections, scan through your power point slides before the presentation and other similar things. Plan the rest of your day! Meditate. If you follow the 5 a.m. principle, you'll get a lot done by 6:30 a.m., probably more than people manage to do in half their day.

Chapter Eight: You are Your Biggest Investment!

"Rich people have small TVs and big libraries and poor people have small libraries and big TVs." — Zig Ziglar

The successful realize that there is no bigger investment than investing in themselves! They will seldom burn themselves out by doing everything they can. They will use every given opportunity to enhance their skills, find promising investment opportunities, brush up on their learning, and spend time in the pursuit of constructive activities that add value to their overall goals. Remember, you can determine a person's personality and mentality to a large extent by observing how they utilize their spare time.

Here are some ways the successful invest in themselves:

1. **They don't indulge time killers.** While the poor are busy watching television, only 9 percent of the rich view reality shows. Compare this with 78 percent of poor folks. Rich people utilize their time more productively. They spend time reading books on wealth, investment, self-development, psychology, business, social and communication skills and anything that enhances their knowledge

and gives them an edge, while interacting with the world at large. The wealthy have an insatiable curiosity for how things can be made more efficient. They will invest in knowledge and skills that make them wiser and more marketable. The learning seldom ceases even when they accomplish their financial goals. They continue to learn, grow and flourish while the others play Candy Crush, binge watch Netflix and spend hours with their gaming console.

2. **They attend seminars, networking events and workshops.** The rich attend these events to upgrade their knowledge, abilities, and skills in the personal and professional sphere. They will not leave out any opportunity to hobnob with like-minded people and learn from them.

3. **They work actively on their bucket list.** The successful lot works on their bucket list, while the poor go with the flow. These people will tick off one goal before moving to the next. Also, their list is ongoing. They'll keep adding new goals that inspire them to go even further. If you haven't done it, begin by making a bucket list of one hundred things you want to do in your lifetime, and work on fulfilling them one at a time.

4. **They invest in a mentor or coach whose values align with theirs.** The rich view their coach as their partner in success. A good coach can help to unlock dormant potential and bring out the best in people. A coach will help streamline your efforts and offer you a clear plan to put all your strategies into action to accomplish the success you deserve. When you invest in yourself, you'll open up a plethora of opportunities. If you are an entrepreneur, you'll realize that few people will invest in you if you don't have confidence in yourself. And you'll develop an inexhaustible reserve of confidence only by investing in yourself physically, spiritually, emotionally and financially. This will help you become the most superior version of yourself, which in turn will attract people to you like magnets. Enlist the help of someone who contributes to your holistic development instead of merely putting you on hustler mode to do and accomplish a lot. The "doer" mode should also be accompanied by all-round

growth, development, and nurturing. Does your coach inspire you to create a work-life balance?

5. **They trust their gut feelings and intuition.** When I have ignored my intuition in the past, I have almost always made a decision that I've regretted later. Learn to trust your intuition in your personal and professional life. Give yourself love by trusting your intuition and honoring your gut feeling. Develop practices to get in touch with your inner self frequently. It will help you make decisions with greater clarity and focus. Value your intuition and avoid allowing the feelings, thoughts, and ideas of others to determine the course of your life. It is empowering to be able to tap into your intuition for making smarter and faster decisions.

6. **They focus on constructive ideas.** The rich do everything they can to develop and work on ideas. This can include reading, meditating, talking to like-minded people, visiting inspirational blogs, getting rid of toxic people, taking a class, focusing on creative activities (like signing up for an art class or redecorating a space), learning a new language, or taking up regular hobbies. They encourage activities that increase their creativity.

7. **They build a positive self-perception.** Successful people don't let setbacks define them. Do you operate with a fear of failure that stops you from going after your dreams? You may have come across some failures and disillusionments along the way and given up when a little more effort would've taken to you your dream life.

Let me tell you up-front that a majority of successful folks whose lifestyle, wealth, and success you admire have gone through the grind like you haven't yet! That's what makes them successful. While we witness their glory and good life, we don't see the endless hours of work, disappointments, setbacks, obstacles and failures, which they move past to accomplish their true destiny.

Also, let me tell you that the rich and successful may not necessarily have it any easier. It's not that the water doesn't get choppy when they are sailing. They just learn to readjust their sails and survive instead of giving up and drowning. That is the main difference between the success and failure mentality. You don't resign to your fate after a few obstacles. You simply learn to stick around and overcome them to get on to the path of success.

You may have read the Harry Potter series. Do you know the story of the writer behind it? J.K. Rowling conceived the idea of creating a fictional character for children. As soon as she started work on it, her mother passed away after a prolonged illness. The process of writing her book halted. She plunged into sorrow and depression, a condition none of us ever want to be in. Rowling didn't get any work done during this phase. Later, in a bid to get over her depression, she became an English language instructor in Portugal.

Things seldom go as planned when the going gets tough. Rowling didn't make much headway with writing her book, and instead she got entangled in a series of bad relationships and a failed marriage, with an additional responsibility—her infant daughter to look after. She now had no source of income, no job, no book written, and a daughter to look after on unemployment benefit. It was so bad; the author had to sit for hours in a café close to her home to keep her child warm, since there were no means to keep her house temperature controlled. She wrote while the baby slept in the café.

After drafting the initial chapters, Rowling excitedly sent the manuscript to publishers, only to be refused each time, until she was rejected by twelve publishers. What would you have done had you been in her desperate situation? Simply give up, right? That's where the success mindset comes in. She continued despite being told that the story wasn't enthralling enough to hold the reader's attention. Rowling believed in herself and her creation. In her own words, her mailbox was packed with rejection letters.

Had you been in her place, you would've thought writing isn't for you and given up. After all, twelve renowned publishers can't be wrong, can they? That's where we stumble majorly. We let other people define our abilities and chances of success rather than believing in our true worth. Rowling had faith in her creation! She truly believed in the power of her visions and dreams, and chased them with gusto!

She sent her manuscript to Bloomsbury Publishing, where the editor sat with his eight-year-old daughter while reading it. The girl was visibly enchanted by the story and expressed her desire to read the rest of the book. Bingo, Harry Potter was born! Bloomsbury decided to publish the book, but the editor also told Rowling to get a steady job because according to him, writing fantasy novels for children wasn't a reliable career option.

I know you must be laughing now reading this—thinking what Rowling is worth today. She isn't just one of the richest authors in the world but also has had her books translated into more than 70 languages, and has sold millions of copies across the globe. The author has a current net worth of around $1 billion, from book sales and through movie rights, endorsements, and sponsorships. She is back at this sum, after previously losing her billionaire status by donating an immense amount of money to charities. This for a divorced, poor, rejected, depressed single mother who decided to take charge of her destiny!

Yes, luck may have played a vital role in her success. The daughter of the publisher happened to read her story and was hooked. However, you can't deny that Rowling moved past her circumstances to keep going. She kept going rather than giving up when many of us would have.

That is the success and wealth mindset in a gist!

Few other things define your success as much as your perception of yourself. The wealthy are confident and believe in their abilities. They realize that time is the most important resource, and make the most of their time by investing it in themselves.

Self-discipline involves practicing ace time management skills, and having a knack for seizing challenges and converting problems into opportunities. Successful people lead a balanced life of discipline and self-control by delaying gratification for the bigger picture. They don't seek instant pleasure or gain. Instead they give up smaller pleasures in the short-term to earn long term rewards. They have positive habits such as sleeping early, eating healthy food, leading a physically active and addiction free life, meditating and spending time on creative pursuits.

Again, rich and successful people will never let others dictate their perception of success or define their reality for them. They believe in the power of their goals and keep going. They also have the ability to move beyond criticism. The rich and successful mindset will seldom take criticism personally. Instead, they will use it as the fuel for the fire in their belly. Their detractors will be their biggest motivators because the more they are told they can't do something, the likelier they are to think of ways to do it. As such, they possess an indomitable spirit.

People who live a full life have a secure perception of themselves. They are more proactive in their approach toward their situation and circumstances. Winners accept complete responsibility for their actions rather than blaming other people or circumstances. They realize that you can have a very powerful reason to do something or an excuse not to do it. You can't have both. They will move past things that cannot be controlled, and instead focus on things that are within their realm of control. The biggest factor—they will never quit. Successful people believe they are destined to success, it is only a matter of time before they accomplish their true glory. When the going gets tough, they may change the course of their action, but they'll seldom give up.

8. **They boost their personal brand value.** Companies spend a large amount of time listening to their customer needs, while improving their products and services. They do this to increase their sales and overall all efficiency. You can also undertake continuous product improvement on yourself to increase your overall value as an entrepreneur or employee and differentiate yourself from other

entrepreneurs or employees. Think of yourself are a product. Yes, that is tip number one when it comes to increasing your personal brand value. You are a brand with your own distinguishable features and benefits—all waiting to be upgraded one year after another. Differentiate yourself from others by creating your own, unique personal brand.

You are a work in progress. The day you stop learning, growing and upgrading, your downfall begins. Self-improvement doesn't have to be pricey. My favorite knowledge upgrade tip is to pick one topic a year. For instance, let us say I want to learn everything I can about Facebook advertising. I'll go to the library or look on my Kindle every month, to borrow or download a different title about Facebook advertising, for an entire year. Can you imagine the knowledge you will gain by reading books about a single topic for an entire year? Go slow and steady, and focus on mastering a single topic at a time instead of cramming your head with overflowing information and trying to be a master of all trades. Enjoy the process of learning.

Pick any topic that you want to gain more knowledge or information about. It can be anything from baking to travel photography to project management to conversation skills. Think about how many topics or subjects you'll end up becoming an expert in within the next five to ten years. These tiny yet winsome habits make all the difference in your life and career.

Another top line habit of the rich and successful is that they boost their learning curve through speed reading and learning. Start your day by reading books that are currently relevant to you. They may offer insights about challenges and issues going on in your life currently. Speed reading is believed to be a habit of several successful folks, including George Washington and Abraham Lincoln. It helps for long term success!

I was interviewing candidates to fill a job position. Predictably, they ran me through what they've accomplished in the last few years to become better versions of themselves. On asking one candidate what he'd done to enhance his skills and efficiency in the last few years, he said, "Nothing really, I graduated from university last year and now I am finally done with my education." Goes without saying, he didn't get the job.

Most successful people realize that learning is a continuous and lifelong pursuit. There are tons of inspiring stories about people who get back to college and embark on a completely different career path after raising children. Take the stories of people who've been laid off, owing to downsizing. They go on to obtain training, education and certifications to completely successfully switch careers. The foundation for all your accomplishments is the willingness, flexibility and openness to absorb new knowledge. This is how to increase your personal brand value from time to time.

The more you learn, the more you'll realize how little you know. The best and fastest way to enhance your worth as an entrepreneur or employee is to keep learning and growing. Treat yourself as a competitive market product, and work upon yourself year after year to increase your overall worth. Instead of wishing for everything to be easier, wish that you become better! And the only way to become better is through constant learning.

9. **They spend 15-30 minutes on focused thinking daily.** Building wealth and success takes years of self-discipline, smart financial decisions and perseverance. Tom Corley, a financial planner, spent half a decade interviewing more than 200 wealthy people, a majority of them being self-made millionaires. Their daily habits, among other things, included spending 15-30 minutes on focused thinking.

In his bestseller, *Change Your Habits, Change Your Life,* Corley talks about how rich and successful people manufacture their destiny and good fortune through carefully cultivated lifestyle habits. Several self-made millionaires interviewed by Corley said they take time out to process and reflect upon things currently happening in their lives.

They take time out to think, reflect and contemplate in isolation, for at least fifteen minutes each morning. They tend to reflect on their health, personal relationships and professional acquisitions. Having quiet, contemplative moments are integral to the process of stress reduction. Even something as simple as devoting a couple of minutes for focused breathing helps eliminate stress.

10. **They adopt habits that make them thrifty and self-sufficient.** The wealthy and successful know the value of having a budget, saving money and investing in assets. While the poor mindset thinks, "I can't afford this" or "This is too pricey for me", the rich mindset will think "How I can afford this in future if not now?" While the poor will think they don't have the money to buy their dream car and spend their money on liabilities such as clothes, shoes, designer accessories etc., the rich will invest their money to grow it, and then buy their dream car through returns on their smart investment.

The biggest distinction between the rich and poor mindset is that the poor mindset thinks about working for money, while the rich mindset thinks about making their money work for them. The difference is profound! The rich will use the cash flow from the returns on their assets to fulfill their desires for luxuries rather than using their assets to create liabilities. Get the difference?

There are 80 people on the planet that are together responsible for making money that is equivalent to money made by 3.5 billion across the world. You may think that these 80 people have inherited their money. But only eleven of these people ruling the world's economy have inherited their wealth. Take the example of Warren Buffet. He grew up in a regular, middle class home. However, he was hooked on the business and investment world from a young age. Today, he is valued at $72.3 billion. No one handed this money to him on a platter. He had a rich mindset, and took the actions of the wealthy, while avoiding the poor mindset and actions. Buffet earned his wealth.

The rich save for a rainy day by being thrifty. Ever wondered how people who travel around the world acquire the funds to do so? The truth is, they cut down on plenty of expenses such as eating out and avoid overpriced coffees at cafes, designer clothes, and other unnecessary expenses, to save for their trips. Similarly, the rich and wealthy save and invest their resources in the right assets that bring them even more wealth. They will always invest in appreciating assets instead of flashy cars, smartphones, and designer clothes that depreciate in value.

Another big factor that differentiates the wealthy and poor mindsets is that the rich mindset believes in prioritizing their expenses. Learn to identify expenses that can be avoided if you don't want to end up in a huge debt. Many poor mindset people will keep buying things they don't need and then sell the things they really need to pay off the debt they built by buying useless things.

Remember, a penny saved is a penny earned. If you save a few hundred dollars by flying business class instead of first class, you can use those dollars to acquire a few assets over a period of time or invest it wisely. The returns of this can be used to fund your expenses. This way you are not working for money but making money work for you.

11. **They avoid getting into a guilt loop.** The most unfortunate thing about not getting much done is that it creates an unfortunate circle or loop of guilt and regret, leading to even more procrastination. Once you realize that you've been putting something off, forgive yourself and get your act together. Stop killing yourself about the past.

Avoid thinking, "I should've tackled this earlier" or "I am always procrastinating" or "I don't manage to get anything done because I am a big loser." This makes things worse. Research has proven that forgiving yourself for past procrastination prevents you from putting off tasks for later. Your sense of accountability will increase, and you'll end up getting more done.

If you are overcome by the guilt and regret of not doing much in the past, you'll stay in that space. However, if you forgive yourself and let yourself know that there's still time to get your act together, you have a good chance of channeling your efforts productively.

I'd go a step ahead and say use past procrastination to your benefit. How can that be done? Well, identify what made you avoid productive tasks. Fear, exhaustion, stress, lack of direction, zero accountability? Address these challenges in the future. For example, if you realize that lack of accountability was the primary reason why you were unable to get stuff done, get an accountability buddy or build an accountability blog. If it is fear of failure that led you into procrastination, what are the steps you'll take to experience less fear and feel more empowered the next time? You can post your goals on social media and share your milestones and progress as and when you accomplish them.

Identifying the cause of past failure is the key to taking action to avoid procrastination in future. Watch out for your negative self-talk. Avoid using terms and phrases such as "need to", "must do" or "have to". These suggest that you don't have a choice, and end up making you feel more disempowered. Instead, try saying, "I choose to". It will change how you feel about the task. You'll feel more empowered and in control of the workload.

12. **They use "mindful patience" as a success strategy.** In a frenzied era where everyone is focusing on getting things done quickly, and most successful businessmen from the late Steve Jobs to Mark Zuckerberg tilt toward creating and breaking previous records, or progress fast, the world has become too competitive for our own good. This fast-pace is at the cost of our sanity and balance! Matilda Ho, an Asian entrepreneur and TED Fellow talks about the concept of "mindful patience" and how she gained considerable success by moving slowly yet steadily. Her philosophy is the complete antithesis of American entrepreneurship that is huge on cranking things out fast. Begin fast, test things fast, upgrade them fast. Rinse. Repeat. When everything around you is so big on "fast",

won't slowing down make you lose out? Heck no, you'll conserve your best for last. Trust me, you'll last longer. When the fast have drained their resources, and their energy is sapped, you'll still be going by adopting a moderate pace. Of course, the fast are also slated for success. But, "mindful patience" will probably sustain you longer over a period of time. A majority of successful ventures and projects that take off overnight actually require years of effort, commitment and restructuring to materialize. They are often built on a weak foundation. When the foundation is weak, the structure resting on top is at a risk of tumbling anytime. Plus, it takes years to make structures with a strong foundation formidable. Contrast this philosophy with the "mindful patience" philosophy. "Mindful patience", as Ho describes it, is about understanding "How to act when you are waiting. It is patience with intention and persistence." How can the philosophy of "mindful patience" be used in entrepreneurship? It is all about aggressive listening and unrelenting learning for building a strong foundation or creating your arsenal bag ready. In effect, you are readying yourself to seize an opportunity when it arises. When the foundation is strong and you've armed yourself for the opportunity, you can make the most of it. You are taking every step necessary to position yourself for success, even when the process takes a while. The waiting time is patiently used to equip yourself for the opportunity whenever it arrives.

Is this the same as slowing down? You are not slowing down really. You are merely creating a culture and lifestyle that facilitates a great habit of learning and reinforcing the lessons, so you can keep improving continuously.

In reality, success does not come fast. It follows a typical sequence of tiny events and accomplishments that seem to take forever. Success also includes some disappointments on the way, and challenges us and our courage, abilities, stamina, integrity, and determination to the core. It tests our willingness to keep going. If we focus on what doesn't work, guess what? We come from a space of frustration and aggravation as our mind is always occupied with what is wrong around us. We may deal with plenty of negative thoughts such as "I am bad at this," or "This won't work," or "There's something seriously wrong with me". When you don't experience success at the expected time, these thoughts prove even more counterproductive. They delay and push your success even further away.

Since we attract what we are feeling, then negative experiences, individuals and outcomes, will attract even higher negative experiences, individuals and outcomes. You'll be stuck in an unfortunate loop. The best way to break free from this is to focus on what you are doing *right*, instead of what is not working in your favor. Spend time learning what is important when it comes to fulfilling a goal, and then focus on everything you are doing right to get there.

Patience will be your biggest virtue on the route to success. Keep at it without looking for instant fixes. Remember, the stronger your foundation, the more solid and infallible your structure is bound to be. When you keep going at a slow yet steady pace, you are building momentum, which ultimately results in you being merely a day, week, or month away from your goal or ultimate success.

Keep in mind that grateful people almost always reflect on what is working as opposed to their failures. They will do more of what is working and change their approach about things that are not. Reflect on everything that is working for you and keep taking action to build your self-discipline and the success will build momentum. At times, the biggest reason why we cannot move ahead is because deep within we do not think we are actually capable of accomplishing our dreams or that we deserve the success we yearn for. If you have self-limiting beliefs or negative views holding you back from accomplishing your goals, take some time to pin down these negative thoughts or self-beliefs. Then turn them on their head to convert them into empowering ideas.

Conclusion

Thank you for downloading *Self Discipline: The Unconventional Guide to Unstoppable Focus, Mental Toughness, Willpower and Building Daily Habits that Will Boost Your Self-Esteem, Beat Procrastination and Maximize Productivity.*

I hope it was able to help you develop an unconventional mindset about self-discipline, getting rid of procrastination, and how to increase your productivity and chances of success. There are plenty of real, practical and actionable tips, which you can begin using right away. I have included multiple action plans, practical pointers and established techniques for increasing your self-discipline muscle, which can help you to achieve your goals in a steady yet solid manner. Remember, when the foundation is strong, the structure stands tall and solid. A weak foundation only leads to a weaker structure, however fast you build the foundation!

This book is packed with valuable hacks to build self-discipline and set you on the path to sustainable success.

The next step is to take action. A person who reads and does not take action is not very different from someone who cannot read. Acquisition of knowledge is not key, implementation is! Information without action is futile. You have to go out there and practice self-discipline to make it work. People often ask me, "Do these tips really work?" I reply with, "Do you have it in you to make them work?" Nothing works if you don't make it work—it's that simple. Only metal that goes through rough conditions becomes gold!

Do everything that it takes to reach your goals through the correct mindset, solid self-discipline strategies, efficient goal setting, time management, positive habits, perseverance, a strong will, and resilience. The steering wheel of your life is in your hands.

Here's to a more productive and self-disciplined life!

Check out another book by Charles Golden

Printed in Poland
by Amazon Fulfillment
Poland Sp. z o.o., Wrocław

56260507R00061